DANNY ROBINS

Danny Robins is an award-winning writer, broadcaster and journalist. In 2021, he created *The Battersea Poltergeist*, a podcast series that combined drama and documentary to tell a real-life ghost story, starring Toby Jones and Dafne Keen. It became a global phenomenon – the #1 Drama Podcast across the whole world.

Danny's first stage play, *Rudy's Rare Records*, was co-commissioned by Birmingham Rep and Hackney Empire ('A wonderful, funny, humane play' *Daily Telegraph*). The follow-up was the acclaimed *End of the Pier*, at London's Park Theatre ('A tour de force' *Sunday Times*). *2:22 – A Ghost Story* marked his West End debut. His first radio drama, *The Most Wanted Man in Sweden*, was nominated for the Writers' Guild's Tinniswood Award.

He has created and written various shows for TV and radio, including the BAFTA-nominated hit series *Young Dracula* for BBC1, and *Rudy's Rare Records* and *The Cold Swedish Winter* for BBC Radio 4. He also created the *Haunted* podcast series for Panoply, and *Uncanny* for BBC Sounds, both of which explore real-life ghost stories.

He grew up in Newcastle-upon-Tyne and now lives with his family in Walthamstow, London.

www.dannyrobins.com

Danny Robins

2:22

A Ghost Story

NICK HERN BOOKS
London
www.nickhernbooks.co.uk

A Nick Hern Book

2:22 – A Ghost Story first published in Great Britain in 2021 as a paperback original by Nick Hern Books Limited, The Glasshouse, 49a Goldhawk Road, London W12 8QP

Cover image: Muse Creative

Designed and typeset by Nick Hern Books, London
Printed in the UK by Mimeo Ltd, Huntingdon, Cambridgeshire PE29 6XX

A CIP catalogue record for this book is available from the British Library

ISBN 978 1 83904 028 3

Introduction
Danny Robins

Do you believe?

We live in an age well attuned to the incendiary power of words, but there's one word that has more power to divide than most – 'ghost'. In our jaded been-there, done-that, unshockable world, the statement 'I have seen a ghost' still has the power to silence a room and forever change the way you see someone, or how people see you. If you're a sceptic, how would you react to your partner claiming the house is haunted? If you're a believer, how would it feel to be told by someone you love that the ghost you saw doesn't exist?

I've been fascinated by ghosts since I was a child. I think it had something to do with growing up in a devoutly atheist family, wondering if there was some other realm where magic existed, if only I believed enough. Some people might have found God, but I found spooks. Fuelled by horror movies, a scream-filled trip to see *The Woman in Black*, and the now-legendary Usborne book, *World of the Unknown: Ghosts* – certain pages too frightening to look at even in a well-lit school library – my interest grew and, as an adult, it became entwined with a realisation of my own mortality. The idea that death was not the end seemed attractive, but did I actually believe? No... well, maybe... but ghosts remained an abstract to be enjoyed in books and films, until a good friend of mine told me she had seen one. I found her account simultaneously impossible and yet totally convincing. It struck me that a ghost sighting is a detective story, where both the witness and ghost are suspects. It lays our relationship with the teller bare. Do we trust them as they reveal this life-changing moment of profound fear? What are the implications if we cannot? The idea for the play was born...

I've spent a lot of the past few years interviewing people who are convinced they've seen ghosts. It began as research for *2:22*, but the stories I collected soon took on a life of their own, spawning two podcast series, *Haunted* and then *The Battersea Poltergeist* for the BBC. I am now sent a steady stream of emails from people who believe they've had paranormal experiences. In some cases, the sender hasn't told anyone before, for fear of being mocked or having their sanity questioned. Being haunted has become a taboo. The stories can be powerful, terrifying, and sometimes deeply moving. Many of the experiences can, I think, be explained, but there are a healthy minority that defy easy answers. These are the ones that set my pulse racing.

So, do ghosts actually exist? Paranormal experiences have followed certain patterns throughout history. Reports of poltergeists haven't changed since Roman times – they thump on walls and throw objects across rooms. Believers cite this as a body of evidence, whilst sceptics see it as the contagion of belief. What I think it proves more than anything, though, is how much humans need ghosts; how deeply rooted and hard to shift they are in our psyche; the supernatural equivalent of Japanese knotweed. There's a reason that, despite all our advances in science, we haven't ever consigned ghosts to the scrapheap of redundant superstition along with elves and unicorns.

Supernatural belief goes through boom periods. After both world wars, there was a mass fascination with seances and spiritualism, as society struggled to process the chaos and loss of life. Now, our own uncertain, death-filled times are breeding a new paranormal renaissance. Horror is hugely popular on film and TV, there's a vogue for spooky podcasts like mine, and the ghost story is again an admired literary form. In the real world, there's also a worrying resurgence in exorcisms in both the Christian and Islamic faiths.

A sceptic might see this as a sign of the times – irrationality and naked belief triumphing over science and rationalism – but it's possible to read it in a different way: not a symptom of chaos but our response to it; a collective longing for magic and hope in a world that feels bleak and cruel. This is the paradox of ghost belief – something so redolent with death is also deeply comforting. Ghost stories, by exposing us to the exhilaration of terror in a contained way, reinforce the security of our own existence. They're our defence against humankind's greatest enemy, death; a way of processing the horrible thought that one day we and all we love will simply cease, our grand achievements rendered meaningless.

Perhaps sceptics need to be careful what they wish for in wanting to dissolve spooky shadows under the powerful floodlights of reason. Whether we believe in them or not, ghosts are society's buffer between life and death, and a world without them – with every corner, nook and cranny illuminated leaving nowhere for the dead to hide, or for us to hide from death – that is a truly frightening idea. Perhaps the question is not 'Do ghosts exist?', but 'Can *we* exist without ghosts?'

2:22 – A Ghost Story was first performed at the Noël Coward Theatre, London, on 11 August 2021 (previews from 3 August), produced by Tristan Baker and Charlie Parsons for Runaway Entertainment, Isobel David and Kater Gordon. The cast and creative team were as follows:

JENNY	Lily Allen
LAUREN	Julia Chan
SAM	Hadley Fraser
BEN	Jake Wood
COMPANY	Richard Pryal
	Bianca Stephens
Director	Matthew Dunster
Set Designer	Anna Fleischle
Costume Designer	Cindy Lin
Lighting Designer	Lucy Carter
Sound Designer	Ian Dickinson for Autograph
Casting Director	Jessica Ronane CDG CSA
Illusions	Chris Fisher
Fight Director	Rachel Bown-William and
	Ruth Cooper-Brown of
	RC Annie Ltd
Vocal/Dialect Coach	Hazel Holder
Production Manager	Marty Moore
Assistant Director	Isabel Marr
Associate Set Designer	Liam Bunster
Associate Casting Director	Abby Galvin
Associate Illusionist	Will Houstoun

For my children Leo and Max,
and my wife Eva, who's too scared to read this

Characters

JENNY, *thirties, a primary-school teacher*
LAUREN, *late thirties, Californian, a psychotherapist*
BEN, *forties, London accent, a builder*
SAM, *late thirties, a physics professor and writer*

PC MILLER, *female*
PC STIRLING, *male*

Setting

The action takes place across twenty-four hours in a house in a
newly gentrified part of London.

Writer's Note

A forward slash (/) in the text indicates the point at which the
next speaker interrupts.

*This text went to press before the end of rehearsals and so may
differ slightly from the play as performed.*

ACT ONE

Scene One

*A Victorian terraced house in the midst of renovation. There's a
spacious open-plan kitchen and dining room, the result of a new
extension. It's fresh, shiny; IKEA supplemented with more
expensive items.*

*A simple old wooden dining table is surrounded by four chairs.
Further away are a sofa, coffee table, beanbag and white rug,
strewn with baby toys. There are framed pictures of a baby on
a shelf.*

*There's a door to a guest toilet – sink and cupboards visible –
and another door to the hall, through which we see recently
polished floorboards and stairs.*

*The upstage wall bridges the extension and the original house.
The new side is taken up by imposing glass doors looking onto a
dark garden. Near the doors is a telescope on a stand. The rest of
the wall is midway through being painted white. There are
stubborn remnants of twee 1970s wallpaper.*

*JENNY is standing on a stepladder, painting, wearing pyjamas,
a fleece jacket and scarf. On the floor is an assortment of paint
tins, rollers, etc.*

*On the kitchen counter is a baby monitor, green lights flickering,
registering the ambient noise of a sleeping baby.*

*There's a large digital clock on the wall. The red numbers
change to 02:20…*

*JENNY stops and comes down the ladder. She pours some white
spirit into a jar and puts her brush into it. There's a glass of red
wine on the floor. She finishes it and turns off the light, then takes
her glass to the kitchen, putting it in the dishwasher –*

*Outside, a security light lurches on, illuminating the garden and an
old shed, making her jump. She looks through the glass – nothing.*

The security light goes out. It's dark again; only the spill from the hall. She walks towards the door – suddenly, the tinny, computerised sound of 'Old MacDonald' punctures the silence –

JENNY. Fuck!

She's stepped on a child's toy. She picks it up, flicks a switch – the music stops. The clock changes to 02:21. She takes a breath, her heart thumping, and walks out of the room –

We hear her walk upstairs. Then, through the monitor, a bedroom door creaks open, followed by the whimper of a baby, mid-dream, and JENNY*'s soothing voice –*

(*Offstage.*) Sssh! It's okay, baba... It's okay.

We hear JENNY *leave the room, then the monitor emits the beeps that show it's run out of battery and goes dead.*

A long beat... The clock changes to 02:22. Another beat, then the silence is torn apart by JENNY *screaming, loud and awful.*

Blackout.

The red numbers of the digital clock sear themselves into the dark.

Scene Two

In the darkness, the clock races forwards to 20:36. Lights up.

The toilet door is now closed. LAUREN *is standing in the kitchen, holding a glass of wine and inexpertly poking a pan of risotto with a wooden spoon. She's dressed up for dinner but cool and casual.*

The baby monitor is on the counter next to her. Through it, we hear SAM *reading* We're Going on a Bear Hunt *by Michael Rosen.*

LAUREN *listens, hooked by the rhythmic flow of* SAM*'s voice, as* JENNY *enters, in a dress and heels.*

SAM *gets to the point in the story where the family have tiptoed into the cave and spotted something in the dark…* JENNY *turns the monitor off.*

LAUREN. I was enjoying that.

JENNY. Sorry.

(*Then.*) Spoiler alert – it's a bear.

An awkward beat. JENNY *picks up the stepladder.*

Phoebe doesn't understand a word of it. But you know what Sam's like. She'll have a PhD by the time she's three.

She's managed to pick up the paint tins too and tries to open the patio door –

Sorry – it's a tip.

LAUREN *helps open the door.*

LAUREN. It's so not.

JENNY *lugs the ladder and paint to the shed.*

JENNY (*from garden*). There's still loads to do!

LAUREN. We could have rescheduled.

JENNY *comes back in – banging her arm on the patio door as she passes.*

JENNY. Ow! I told Sam to tidy.

LAUREN. When did he get back?

JENNY. An hour ago. No fucking warning he'd be late.

She shuts the door. An awkward beat – neither quite knowing what to say next.

He'll be down soon.

LAUREN (*trying hard*). You look good.

JENNY *starts to pick up baby toys from the rug, putting them into a toybox.*

JENNY. I look tired.

(*Noticing a spot on her dress*.) And stained.

(*Scratches at it*.) Paint.

LAUREN. Fuck.

She pours JENNY *a glass of wine*.

JENNY (*crossing to check*). How's the risotto?

LAUREN. I gave it a few prods.

She hands JENNY *the glass*.

JENNY. Thanks.

She sips.

LAUREN. Ben chose it. / Sorry.

JENNY. It's fine.

She spots another toy and picks it up – a teddy bear.

'Mister Bear'. / She loves it.

LAUREN. I never know what to send. It was him or tequila.

JENNY *puts the bear on a shelf*.

JENNY. God, not while I'm feeding.

(*Relaxing slightly*.) Can you imagine? Breast-milk slammers.

LAUREN. Can't believe I haven't met her yet.

JENNY. Sorry.

LAUREN. It's me. I've been so busy. / Lots of new patients…

JENNY. No. It's our fault. The first year, you know how it is…

LAUREN. Not really.

The toilet flushes.

JENNY. We don't see anyone. Just other people with babies.

LAUREN. Breeders.

JENNY *stirs the risotto*.

You must be desperate to get back to work? / Or not?

JENNY. I miss the pupils. Having your own kid's way more stressful.

She spots one last toy, on the kitchen floor, and picks it up. It squeaks.

Sometimes I pretend I need a poo, just so I can hide in there.

LAUREN. I've done that at work. A particularly tricky patient…

They smile, some of the previous tension eased, as the toilet door opens and BEN *bursts out. Like* LAUREN, *he's dressed up for the occasion, but his clothes are far more conventional.*

BEN. Well, Jenny, your toilet…

JENNY. Oh / dear…

BEN. Is an absolute beauty.

LAUREN. Ben does bathrooms.

JENNY. Yes, I / heard.

BEN. Quality tiling. Nice sink. Lovely action on that flush. Who did it?

JENNY. Oh… Sam knows… They're Albanian.

BEN. Ah, right. Cheap I / guess?

LAUREN (*pouring him a glass of wine*). Stop grilling her.

BEN. Well, it's bloody gorgeous, pardon my French. Give it a go, Lauren. Have a wee.

LAUREN (*handing him the glass*). / Maybe later.

BEN. That soap!

LAUREN crosses to sit on the sofa.

'Honey, lavender, and goat's milk'. Actual goat soap! It was a pleasure to wash my hands.

(*Joins* LAUREN *on the sofa.*) I did it twice.

LAUREN. Ben doesn't get out much.

SAM enters, in scruffy jeans and an old T-shirt. Unlike the others, he's made no effort to smarten up.

SAM. Loz!

LAUREN. Sammy!

She springs up. He kisses her on the cheek.

SAM. Sorry, she took a while to nod off.

LAUREN. Ben – Sam. Sam / – Ben.

BEN stands awkwardly and they shake hands –

SAM. / Hello, mate.

BEN. Pleasure.

JENNY places a wine glass down for SAM.

JENNY. Was everything okay?

BEN fills SAM's glass.

BEN. Dive in.

SAM. Thanks, mate.

BEN. You're playing / catch-up!

SAM (*to JENNY*). She's fine! I haven't been away that long! Jenny worries I might accidentally chuck Phoebe out the window.

(*Goes to kiss her.*) And yes, I closed it.

She evades him and turns on the monitor.

JENNY. He's convinced Phoebe needs 'fresh air'.

(*Listening for Phoebe's breathing.*) You'll learn Sam's the world expert on parenting.

LAUREN. Does he still say it?

SAM (*sitting on sofa*). What?

LAUREN. Your catchphrase.

(*Mimicking him.*) 'I think you'll find!'

(*To BEN.*) University quiz team. Every fricking time you'd hear –

(*Clears throat, 'Sam' impression*.) ' It's the Battle of Culloden, 1746, I think you'll find.'

SAM. 1745. I think you'll find.

LAUREN (*laughs*). Same old Sam! I even had it printed on a T-shirt. You never wore it.

SAM. I think you'll find I did. Student Union Quiz Night, grand final. You were too pissed to notice. Same old Loz.

LAUREN *looks hurt.* JENNY *puts a bowl of olives on the coffee table.*

JENNY. I'm sorry if it's cold. Our boiler's playing up.

BEN *grabs a handful of olives.*

It's typical. You're our first / guests.

LAUREN. It's perfect, Jenny. You guys have done so well. / Haven't they?

BEN (*eating*). / Lovely yeah.

SAM. It was the first house we saw.

JENNY. I wasn't sure, but / Sam…

SAM. I knew.

BEN (*still eating*). Good area too.

He puts his stones into the bowl.

LAUREN. Ben used to live round here.

BEN. As a kid. Back in the Dark Ages. Wasn't like it is now – cycle lanes and tapas bars. Bet this cost a bit?

JENNY (*shoots a look at* SAM). I think we should have paid more. It belonged to a widow. She'd lived here forty years. And her husband's family before that.

SAM. She wanted to find the right people she said.

JENNY. To look after it.

LAUREN. It's so big!

SAM. Room for four. We're trying again.

LAUREN (*surprised, not sure how to respond*). Right.

BEN. Big job?

   (*Off their looks.*) I mean with the house.

SAM. Huge. It was like a museum to this woman's terrible taste. Seventies wallpaper, thick carpets. Everything was brown or beige.

JENNY. Poor Margaret. It was full of all these things her husband had made. Rickety wardrobes and wonky shelves.

SAM (*mimics 'Margaret', Cockney*). 'Oooh, he was good with his hands, my Frank. Could knock up anything. Cupboards, shelves, even the next-door neighbour…'

JENNY. Sam!

SAM. Sorry, but she was weird!

JENNY. She was sad. Can you imagine what it felt like? Living here alone, surrounded by…

   (*To* LAUREN, *seeking some empathy*.) You know…

LAUREN. Gaps?

JENNY. Yes! Frank-shaped gaps. All his tools are in the shed. Like this neat little shrine.

SAM. She made me promise to / use them!

JENNY. It was like the whole house was… missing someone.

SAM. Cheerful. Anyway, we ripped it all out. Knocked through. Made it ours.

   (*Gestures to the hall.*) Have a look round –

BEN. You sure?

SAM. You can peep in on Phoebe, Loz.

LAUREN (*smiles awkwardly*). Yeah…

   She and BEN *exit to the hall.* SAM *waits for the door to shut, then crosses to* JENNY.

SAM (*sotto*). Well, I don't think much of him.

JENNY. He's nervous.

(*Re his clothes.*) You could have changed.

SAM (*looking at wine bottle, sarcastic*). That wine he brought / looks nice.

JENNY. The paint was still out.

SAM. You know he did her bathroom?

JENNY. Oh God, the bloody white spirit.

She's spotted the white spirit bottle on the floor.

SAM. Don't you think that's weird? Hooking up with your own builder?

She picks the bottle up.

JENNY. Not really. Gynaecologist maybe. Builder no.

(*Re: white spirit.*) Fuck it – I'm sticking it in here.

She puts it on top of the cupboard in the toilet.

SAM. It's a bit Lady Chatterley.

JENNY *crosses to the kitchen to start putting a salad together.*

I think Lauren's having an early mid-life crisis. Hitting forty and bonking builders.

JENNY. You never like her boyfriends.

SAM. No?

(*Then.*) You alright?

JENNY. I'm tired, Sam.

SAM. Not going to get any easier. I heard someone say the difference between having one kid and two is like the difference between owning a pet and running a zoo.

She half-laughs grudgingly. He puts his arms out and she lets him hug her, looking through the patio doors.

You can see the Plough tonight.

JENNY. Why were you so late?

SAM. It was a difficult journey.

>*(Tightens his hug, seductively.)* Let's make another baby.
>After they've gone.

JENNY. Your hands are cold.

>*She breaks the embrace, going back to her salad.*

SAM *(gazing proudly)*. God I bloody love these doors.

JENNY. There's too much glass.

SAM. Are you mad?

JENNY. Mum said it feels like someone's out there, watching.

SAM. She's a Catholic. She always thinks someone's watching.

>*(Then.)* I have this vision of us. Sitting here with the telescope
>and mugs of cocoa.

>*She meets his gaze.*

>I missed you. So much. Both of you.

JENNY. But not enough to call?

SAM. I lost my bloody phone!

>*(Gently.)* Look, I know it's not been easy…

>*There's a whimper through the baby monitor.* JENNY *tenses –*

JENNY. She's –

SAM *(gently)*. Asleep.

>*They listen for a beat, waiting for Phoebe's breathing to
>return to normal.*

>You did the right thing. Putting her back in her room. Now
>I'm home…

>*Another murmur from Phoebe, relaxing into sleep.*

>Trust me. It will stop.

>BEN *and* LAUREN *come back in.*

LAUREN. Oh my God! It makes my flat look like a shoebox.

SAM. It's a work-in-progress.

LAUREN. You should talk to Ben.

BEN. They might not want that, Lauren.

But he's already finding a business card.

SAM. No, I mean, it's hard to find good / people.

BEN. Here's my card.

He puts it on the coffee table.

JENNY. / Thanks.

SAM. Hey, is it too light in here? Watch this, Loz – (*Talks to an Alexa device on the counter.*) Alexa, dim the dining-room lights!

There's no response.

Oh bollocks!

JENNY. Say it louder – 'Alexa, dim the dining-room lights!'

ALEXA. Okay.

The lights dim. JENNY *takes out plates and cutlery.*

SAM. You should get one, Loz. Helps with all kinds of stuff.

LAUREN. That's why I got Ben.

JENNY (*to* SAM). Can you set the table?

JENNY *puts the plates and cutlery on the table, removing the fruit bowl.*

BEN. I'll do that!

LAUREN (*re: table*). Is this new?

BEN *starts to set the table.*

SAM. / God no!

JENNY. Margaret left it. It's one of Frank's.

SAM (*putting on his 'Margaret' voice*). 'I couldn't fit it in me new bungalow.'

JENNY (*shooting him a look*). Poor Margaret. She's only my mum's age.

LAUREN. How is your mum?

JENNY. Missing us. The old flat was so close / to them.

BEN (*setting table, to* SAM). Lauren said you've been away?

SAM. Yeah. On Sark.

JENNY (*to* LAUREN). She's distracting / herself.

SAM (*off* BEN*'s blank look*). One of the Channel Islands.

JENNY. Planning the christening.

SAM. Oh no, is she still banging on about that?

(*To Ben.*) It's the only island in the world with dark-sky status.

JENNY. Phoebe's nearly one! I'm going to send out invites.

BEN. Dark sky?

SAM. Invitations. You 'invite' somebody, by sending an 'invitation'.

LAUREN. I think you'll / find!

SAM (*to* BEN). It means no light pollution. Perfect place to view the stars.

JENNY. Perfect place to run away. Not call your family.

BEN. You into that then? Stars?

LAUREN. Sam's writing a book.

SAM. 'Astronomy for Idiots'. My attempt to explain the universe in a way that will fill stockings next Christmas.

LAUREN. Listen to him, sounding like he doesn't care. Years of teaching spotty undergrads and finally he's been asked to write something people might actually read.

JENNY. Anyway, expect a fucking invite, Lauren. You too, / Ben.

SAM. Fine, but I'm hanging out for a repeat of the wedding.

(*To* BEN.) Full Catholic service. As we say our vows, the church gets hit by lightning.

LAUREN (*laughs at the memory*). It's true!

SAM. Jen's mum turns to her dad and says...

He sets her up for the punchline –

JENNY (*puts on Irish accent, points to God*). 'I told you he wasn't happy.'

They laugh – the tension easing a bit. JENNY *puts the salad on the table.*

BEN. You're not religious then?

SAM. No. You?

BEN. Nah.

SAM. Phew.

BEN. I mean, I'm spiritual. I believe in something.

SAM. Like...?

BEN. Well, nothing weird. Just, I believe my mum's up there, you know, looking down on me.

JENNY. Really?

BEN. As an angel.

SAM. Blimey.

BEN. And I believe in reincarnation. I know I've lived before.

JENNY. Sam –

SAM. Holy fuck.

JENNY. Can you grate / parmesan?

SAM. When?

BEN. What?

SAM. When did you live before?

BEN (*unsure if he should say*). The French Revolution.

SAM stifles a laugh.

SAM. Sorry, mate! It's just, it's always somewhere romantic, isn't it? Paris 1789, Hastings 1066. Never 1980s Wolverhampton.

JENNY. Food in five!

BEN (*feeling mocked*). I might have a quick fag. / If that's…

JENNY. Oh… course.

She opens the patio door.

BEN. Filthy habit. Lauren's trying to reprogramme me.

LAUREN. What's that smell?

JENNY. Foxes. There's a den somewhere.

BEN *walks out and the security light comes on.*

SAM. Thought the builders might've scared them off, but they're stubborn sods. We saw this documentary –

JENNY. There was a fox who mugged a man. He was walking home.

SAM. From Sainsbury's –

JENNY. And it cornered him –

SAM. Trying to steal his shopping!

JENNY. He had to fight it off with a garlic baguette.

SAM. They're nature's hoodies.

BEN *lights his cigarette.*

BEN (*to* LAUREN). You coming out?

LAUREN. Nah. I don't want to get eaten.

She shivers and goes to close the door.

SAM (*to* BEN, *re: door*). They haven't put the handle on yet, so knock if you want to come in.

LAUREN *shuts the door.*

LAUREN. Think I'll use the bathroom. Since it's had such good reviews.

She goes into the toilet. SAM *crosses to* JENNY, *who's grating parmesan.*

SAM (*sotto*). He's worse than I thought! When he said he was reincarnated…! Holy shitting Bernard!

JENNY. He may have hidden depths.

SAM. He hides them extremely well.

The security light clicks off and BEN *is hidden by darkness.*

JENNY. You always do this.

SAM. What?

JENNY. Talk, whilst I do everything.

She opens the cupboard to take out water glasses.

SAM. I'm just saying – it's going to be a long night. Like, what do we even chat about? 'So, Louis the Sixteenth? For or against?'

As JENNY *takes the glasses out, a padded envelope falls from the cupboard.*

What's that?

JENNY *picks it up.*

JENNY (*guarded*). Mum brought it round.

She opens it and pulls out a crucifix.

SAM. Christ.

JENNY. Well spotted. It's the one I had growing up.

SAM. What are we supposed to do with it?

JENNY. Put it in Phoebe's room.

Beat. The toilet flushes.

SAM. Send it back.

JENNY. Not till we've talked / about this.

SAM. I thought we did.

JENNY. Right. I just couldn't hear myself over your voice.

LAUREN *comes out of the bathroom.* JENNY *quickly puts the crucifix back into the envelope and puts it in the cupboard.*

LAUREN. Ben was right about that soap. I feel like I just gentrified my hands.

JENNY *lifts the risotto off the hob.*

JENNY. We should eat.

LAUREN *opens the patio door.*

LAUREN. Ben!

(*Then, sotto.*) Sammy?

SAM. Yes?

LAUREN. Give him a chance.

SAM. You know me.

LAUREN. Exactly.

BEN *enters as* JENNY *brings the risotto to the table.*

BEN. Sorry!

He closes the door.

The window. In your daughter's room. It was open.

SAM. It's not.

BEN. The one with the kids' curtains? It's / wide open.

SAM. It's definitely / not.

JENNY. Sam!

SAM *sighs and goes upstairs.*

BEN. Sorry, I didn't mean to... it's just it's cold tonight.

JENNY *listens to the monitor.*

LAUREN. This looks delicious, Jenny.

BEN. Asparagus, eh? I'll have to brace myself.

(*Off* LAUREN*'s look.*) It makes your pee smell, doesn't it?

(*Off her dismay.*) This is why she doesn't bring me out. Odd though, eh? Do you reckon there's a scientific reason?

JENNY *is still listening to the monitor, her face hard to read.*

LAUREN *is topping up their wine glasses.*

LAUREN (*hovering over* JENNY*'s glass*). Jen?

JENNY (*snapping out of it*). Sorry. Yes.

She starts to serve them, trying to switch mood, be the good host.

(*To* BEN.) It must have changed a lot round here. Since you were a kid?

BEN. Oh, yeah.

(*As she serves him.*) Bit more. Cheers.

(*Then.*) It's layers, isn't it? It was all Cockneys. Then the Asians came. The Poles. And now… nice people, like you. But there's still a little bit of everything. Somewhere underneath.

(*Nods to the wall.*) Like wallpaper.

SAM *comes back down.*

SAM. It was open.

JENNY. You / said…

SAM. I must have forgot…

JENNY. Did you?

SAM. Must have.

(*Off her tense look.*) Oh, don't get like that…

He sits. Through the monitor, Phoebe cries.

BEN. Perfect timing.

JENNY. Did you wake her?

SAM. No! For Christ's sake!

JENNY *heads to the door.*

Leave her a moment!

Phoebe cries again. JENNY *exits upstairs.* SAM *sighs, exasperated.*

LAUREN (*jovially*). Ever wish you hadn't done it?

> *Beat.*

SAM. Had a kid? No. Ever wish you had?

> LAUREN *recoils at this cruelty.*

> (*Instantly regretting.*) Sorry, Loz. That was… I'm tired.

> (*Then.*) How's work?

LAUREN. Oh, depressing. Underfunded.

SAM. Like the whole NHS, I guess.

LAUREN. Yeah, but they seem to care especially little about the mind. If you're recovering from an operation now, they ask you to define your pain on a scale of one to ten. They want us to do the same. 'How serious is your trauma? A four or a five?' Everyone's a 'client'. I've got a fourteen-year-old who tried to set herself on fire. They want to know how long it will take me to 'process her case'.

BEN. Nobody give a toss.

> (*Off* LAUREN*'s surprised look.*) When I was a kid, we were in and out of all the houses on our street. But now, you've got Netflix, Facebook, Amazon, Deliveroo. Who needs people?

SAM. It's this government.

BEN. No it's us. We forgot how to care.

> *Outside, we hear the sound of foxes calling to each other.*

SAM. It's the foxes. At night, when I'm writing, I can hear them running round outside, screaming and fucking.

> *He hasn't touched his food.* BEN *has nearly finished his.*

BEN. Not hungry?

SAM. Not so much. Fancy some music? Alexa, play my dinner-party playlist.

> *Alexa doesn't respond.*

Oh, come on…

LAUREN (*slightly louder*). Alexa, pretty please, play Sam's dinner-party playlist.

ALEXA. Okay.

Music comes on – it's Portishead.

SAM. Jenny's done something to her whilst / I was away…

LAUREN (*re: music*). This tune takes me back. Your uni bedsit. Spliffs and Tesco cava.

SAM. It was my seduction soundtrack. I'd bang this on and get my telescope out.

BEN. Oh yeah?

SAM. The two things no woman can resist – Portishead and an in-depth discussion of the solar system.

LAUREN laughs. JENNY comes back in.

JENNY. The window was open.

SAM. What?

JENNY. It was still open.

SAM. Well I… Is the sash broken?

JENNY. No.

SAM. It must be.

LAUREN (*re: food*). This is so good.

JENNY sits, tension crackling. LAUREN and BEN eat. SAM and JENNY don't.

BEN (*remembering*). Sam… do you know why asparagus makes your pee smell?

SAM (*distracted*). What?

BEN holds up a piece of asparagus on his fork.

It contains a sulphurous compound. When your digestive system breaks it down, it releases / a smell.

JENNY (*blurts out, forcefully*). It's her room!

She puts her cutlery down with a clang. LAUREN *and* BEN *look at her, surprised.*

BEN. Are you okay?

SAM. It's nothing.

(*Off her upset look.*) Really? You want to do this?

(*Sighs, to the others.*) I didn't want to tell you, but… we seem to have a ghost.

Beat, then he laughs. LAUREN *laughs.* JENNY *and* BEN *do not.*

Seriously, I've come home to find the house is haunted.

JENNY. When you say 'haunted', it makes it sound like it's not…

SAM. What?

JENNY. Real.

LAUREN. Sorry? You're not joking? This is actually a thing?

SAM. No…

(*Off* JENNY*'s look.*) Oh come on!

(*Laughs; then.*) I've been away. Jen's been sitting here, new house, in the dark… And Phoebe – she's pretty creepy.

(*Off their looks.*) All babies are. In the nicest possible way. Staring at things that aren't there. Babbling to themselves. / Projectile vomiting.

JENNY. I think I hear a ghost.

LAUREN *freezes, reaching for parmesan.*

LAUREN. Now I really want to know.

SAM. Sweetie, you're going to / look mad.

LAUREN. Alexa, turn the music off.

ALEXA. Okay.

The music stops.

SAM. Oy!

LAUREN. Sssh! Jenny's got the conch.

A long beat as JENNY *decides how best to tell it.*

JENNY. While the builders were here, Phoebe was in with us. But last week, they finally left, so –

SAM. We decided to put her in her own / room.

JENNY. It wasn't ready.

SAM. Needs another lick / of paint.

JENNY. But Sam insisted.

SAM. She's eleven months! All the manuals say it's best for everyone to have their / own space.

JENNY. I had the monitor next to our bed, so if she cried, I could go and / feed her.

SAM. Her room's so close, you barely / need it.

JENNY. The first night, she seemed unsettled.

SAM. She always is.

JENNY. Since we moved here…

SAM. It's developmental…

JENNY. On Tuesday, Sam went on his trip…

SAM. Bad timing. I'd had it booked for months…

JENNY. That night. I woke up. I thought I'd heard my phone, but something was coming through the monitor, and it wasn't Phoebe…

Beat.

I heard footsteps. Someone walking on the floorboards in her room.

LAUREN. / Shit.

BEN. Blimey.

JENNY. I didn't know what to do. I grabbed my phone, thinking – do I call the police?

LAUREN. I would / have.

JENNY. I... I was bricking it. But, I thought – I have to do something. So, I went up to her door...

BEN. Blooming heck.

JENNY. I could still hear it. Loud. Like somebody was walking in a circle. With hard shoes. Round and round and round. Round the cot.

LAUREN. Jesus...

JENNY. So, I... Fuck... This still feels like the bravest fucking thing I've ever done. I pushed open the door and turned on the light, and...

Beat, they hang on her words.

There was no one there.

SAM. It's a well-known fact ghosts are scared of electricity. They're like the Amish.

BEN. Your daughter?

JENNY. Asleep. I could imagine Sam laughing, saying: 'You're knackered, you're hearing things.' And I thought he'd be right. Because I don't believe in ghosts.

BEN. I do.

SAM. Of course you do.

JENNY. I figured it was some stupid dream or... I don't know... my brain. But then... it happened again. The next night.

LAUREN. You're kidding / me?

BEN. The same thing?

JENNY. Yes. And this is the strangest bit. It was at the same time. Cos I'd looked at my phone the first night. And the second. It was 2:22.

SAM. Coincidence.

BEN. What did you do?

JENNY. Tried to call Sam. Again and a-fucking-gain.

LAUREN. Sammy! You let your wife stew in a haunted house?

SAM. This isn't The Exorcist! I'd lost my phone. The one pisser
of a dark-sky island – drop something down a hill, there's no
bloody hope of finding it.

(*To* JENNY, *genuine remorse*.) You know I feel like / shit...

JENNY. So, this is so stupid... I called the police.

SAM *gives an amused groan*.

BEN. What did they say?

JENNY. I have a reference number. 'Somebody will be in touch.'
They thought I was loopy. I probably did too, except...

BEN. It happened again?

JENNY *nods*.

LAUREN. No!!

JENNY. On Thursday. I'd made my mum come over. There was
no way I could sleep. I sat outside Phoebe's room. Mum was
in our bed, but she was just lying awake too. And we both
heard it. At 2:22!

LAUREN. Sam, this is weird!

SAM. You've met her mum...

JENNY. She doesn't believe in ghosts either!

SAM. Apart from the Holy One. And Jesus. Though, technically,
he's a zombie.

JENNY (*fiercely*). Stop it! Stop making it seem / ridiculous...

SAM (*gentler, realising he's gone too far*). I'm sorry. Look...
there are so many things in old houses that make strange
noises... Heating pipes expanding and contracting. Creaky
floorboards. Mice.

BEN. Mice that turn up the same time each night?

SAM (*ignoring him*). It could be electrical. It stopped when you
flicked the light switch, right? So it's some dodgy circuit
ticking behind a wall. Your imagination does the rest. Tick,
clunk, tick... Footsteps.

JENNY. It isn't just footsteps…

Beat.

Last night… I put Phoebe in our bed and I… I decided to stay up again. I wanted to… prove to myself it was real. Before you came home.

SAM *shakes his head in wry bemusement.*

I painted in here and then, at 2:21, I went up to check Phoebe in our room. And then, I went into hers.

LAUREN. God, I can't bear this!

JENNY. A minute later, it came. Walking round and round.

SAM. Tick, clunk…

JENNY. But this / time…

SAM. Tick…

JENNY. I also heard a voice.

SAM (*suddenly thrown*). Sorry? Why didn't you tell me this?

JENNY. Because I knew what you'd say.

SAM. This is completely mental. What would I say?

JENNY. 'This is completely mental.' It was a man's voice.

BEN. Saying what?

JENNY. Nothing. It wasn't words. It was a sound. He… it… was crying.

(*Looks up at them.*) I know how mad this sounds. But I turned on the light, and the room was empty. Just me and Phoebe's empty cot.

There's a whimper from the baby monitor.

But I could feel it. Somebody had just left the room.

SAM. Sweetheart. This is nuts… It didn't…

JENNY. What?

SAM. It was a dream.

JENNY. I wasn't asleep.

SAM. Well…

JENNY. You don't believe / me?

SAM. It's not about / belief…

JENNY. It happened. Four / nights running.

SAM. You've got yourself wound up. Your mum / doesn't help…

JENNY. Do you believe me?

SAM. I should have been / here…

JENNY. Do you believe me?

SAM. Let's move on.

JENNY. Do you believe your wife?!

A charged beat.

SAM (*to* BEN *and* LAUREN). I'm sorry. This is embarrassing / now.

LAUREN. Do you want us to go?

JENNY. No!

SAM. Of course / not.

JENNY. I want you to stay.

SAM. Absolutely.

JENNY. Until 2:22.

A shocked silence.

SAM (*laughing nervously*). Jen!

(*Then.*) You're serious?

JENNY. Yes. I want them to be here.

Phoebe whimpers again…

As witnesses. When you hear it too.

Snap to black.

Scene Three

The clock races forwards in the dark to 22:33.

Lights up.

The remains of dinner are on the table. LAUREN *is on the sofa.* BEN *sits awkwardly on the beanbag. They're both holding wine glasses, staring fixedly at the baby monitor on the coffee table. Through it, we hear footsteps in Phoebe's room.*

The footsteps come downstairs, then the door opens and…

SAM. Boo!

They instinctively flinch.

She's fast asleep. No sign of ectoplasm.

JENNY (*from inside toilet*). I can hear you!

LAUREN (*shivers*). It's got cold.

BEN. You expect it. On a vigil.

SAM. Pardon?

BEN. That's what they call it. When you investigate a haunted house.

The toilet flushes.

SAM. Oh God. Have you done this before?

BEN. A few stately homes. Used to take Mum. You pay your money and they let you stay the night. There's always cold spots. Where the activity is.

SAM. Well, don't get your hopes up, eh? Jenny's got previous.

JENNY *comes out of the toilet.*

JENNY. Excuse me?

SAM. In our last flat, she was convinced our neighbour had murdered his wife.

LAUREN *tops up their wine glasses as he talks.* SAM *declines – his is still full.*

The woman had disappeared and Jen saw the bloke digging a hole in the garden.

JENNY. A really big hole!

SAM. So she called the police, and…?

JENNY. It turned out she'd left him for his friend and his dog had died. Same week. Poor bastard.

She and SAM *laugh together.*

SAM (*affectionate teasing*). The cops are probably building a file on you – nuisance caller.

LAUREN. Don't listen! I'd get freaked out here, alone in the dark. Wondering what's lurking at the bottom of the bed, ready to grab your feet.

She launches herself at SAM's *feet, rather attention-grabbingly – accidentally spilling his wine onto the rug.*

Oh shit!

BEN. / Lauren!!

LAUREN. Sorry!

BEN (*crossing to toilet*). I'll get some toilet paper.

LAUREN (*to* SAM). You got a cloth?

SAM (*looking*). I'll just get –

JENNY *has found a cloth in the kitchen. She hands it to* LAUREN.

JENNY. I wasn't alone.

LAUREN. Sorry?

BEN *returns with handfuls of toilet paper and starts mopping.*

JENNY. You said you'd be scared 'alone here in the dark'. But that's the worst thing. The whole time Sam was away, I've felt… someone else is here.

There's a whimper through the monitor.

SAM. And there she is.

LAUREN *hands* BEN *the cloth, vaguely helping him with the toilet paper.*

LAUREN (*re: monitor*). Doesn't that thing make you paranoid?

SAM. Oh yeah. In the beginning, we were glued to it non-stop, like if we put it down, Phoebe would breathe her last.

JENNY. Don't joke.

SAM. I'm not. That first night we brought her home from hospital, I don't think I've ever been so scared. She stirred once.

JENNY. Wind.

SAM. We sprinted upstairs!

They laugh at the memory.

And the rest of the night we sat by her cot, watching this amazing little creature we had to learn to protect.

(*An ironic nod to* BEN.) A vigil. I challenge anyone to be a parent and not be permanently terrified.

BEN (*finishes mopping*). Good as new.

(*On* LAUREN*'s behalf.*) Sorry about that.

He hands JENNY *the cloth.*

LAUREN *crosses to the toilet to throw the toilet paper away. The door swings shut behind her.*

JENNY (*shivers*). It's freezing, Sam.

She takes a blanket from the sofa and wraps it round herself.

SAM. Can we all agree the ghost has broken the boiler?

JENNY. I do not think that! You sarcastic / twat!

SAM. No, seriously, this is his dastardly plan. First the heating, then the lights, and finally, most terrifyingly of all – the Wi-Fi!

LAUREN *comes out of the toilet.*

JENNY. Alexa, will you protect everyone apart from Sam?

ALEXA. I don't understand the question.

BEN. I could look at the boiler for you?

SAM. Thanks, mate, but it's kaput.

JENNY. They're coming back tomorrow.

BEN. On a Sunday? They work hard, those Albanians. Still, can't hurt if I take a peek?

SAM *shrugs*.

JENNY. Thank you, Ben.

BEN *goes to look at the boiler.* JENNY *starts to clear the table.* LAUREN *sits, listening to the monitor.*

LAUREN. I'm addicted now. Every little rise and fall of breath.

SAM. You know how baby monitors were invented? It'd make a good quiz question. The first model was called the 'Radio Nurse' – they've got one in the V&A. Hit the market back in the thirties, after this famous kidnapping in America. The Lindbergh case. You know it?

JENNY *shakes her head.*

LAUREN. You must! They called it 'the crime of the century'. Charles Lindbergh!

She starts googling it on her phone.

SAM. He was the first guy to fly non-stop over the Atlantic. That was like landing on the Moon back then.

LAUREN. He became this big celebrity. Bought a mansion out in...

(*Skim-reading Wikipedia article.*) Yeah. New Jersey... This is 1932. And the kidnappers climbed through a window and took his baby from its bedroom.

JENNY. / Oh God...

SAM. Whilst he and his wife were downstairs.

JENNY. Urgh. They wanted money?

LAUREN. Yeah, and he offered a reward. It went on for months. But the baby was found dead.

JENNY. Jesus. The kidnappers killed it?

SAM. No, they were just morons and it had all gone wrong.

LAUREN (*skimming the gory details on Wikipedia*). Pretty grim.

SAM. And everyone dreaded it happening to their child, so some bright spark came up with the Radio Nurse.

(*Indicates the monitor.*) People felt they had to have one, or they'd be bad parents. It's a product born from paranoia.

JENNY. But if it gave them peace of mind, that's a good thing?

SAM. Except, all the Radio Nurses were on the same frequency, so people heard 'phantom noises' from other monitors. The screams of a child several streets away. Their attempt to ward off the thing they feared most, simply bred more fear.

Beat.

Still happens, by the way.

JENNY. What?

SAM. These can pick up other monitors. There's a good chance your 'ghost' is right here.

He points to the monitor.

LAUREN. Real footsteps, but in someone else's house?

JENNY. At the same time every night?

SAM. Mum or Dad gets back from their night shift, goes to check on their kid, gazing adoringly, as they walk round and round the cot.

LAUREN. He's good.

JENNY. Ingenious. Except I could still hear the footsteps when I went into the room. And the crying. That didn't come through the monitor. It was there, next to me, real, and fucking horrible. So, sorry to piss on your theory, Sherlock, but any other suggestions?

She shuts the dishwasher emphatically. BEN *had crossed to the hall and has now returned.*

BEN. This might sound thick, but does there have to be another explanation? Why can't it be a ghost?

SAM. The laws of thermodynamics. Things cannot appear and disappear.

BEN. In your opinion.

SAM. Well, mine and the entire scientific establishment.

BEN. I won't argue.

JENNY. Oh go on.

LAUREN. He loves it.

Beat.

BEN. I've had experiences I don't think you can explain with science.

SAM. On your 'vigils'?

BEN. Things that have proper freaked me out.

SAM. That's because you're a lizard.

BEN. Sorry?

LAUREN. It's a simplification, but you can say our brains have three parts. The monkey brain governs reason and language. The mouse brain controls desire –

SAM. Hunger.

LAUREN. Love. And, at the bottom is the oldest part – the lizard brain.

SAM. Primal instinct.

LAUREN. It's there to protect us from predators.

SAM. You want to know why 'haunted houses' feel cold? Because when you're scared, your lizard brain diverts blood from your hands and feet to your vital organs. It's not the house that's freezing – it's you. The reason your hairs stand on end? It's trying to trap a layer of air, to keep you warm. There's even a logic to shitting yourself. Covered in your own faeces, you're a less attractive meal.

LAUREN. The interesting thing is that instinct can shut down reason.

SAM. Lizard versus monkey.

LAUREN. Lizard wins.

JENNY. That's what happens when you're scared, but where does it come from?

SAM. Eh?

JENNY. Fear's not a mood, like happiness or sadness. It's a response.

BEN. Bingo! This is what your lot…

SAM. My lot?

BEN. Science people… 'Experts'.

SAM. Oh dear…

BEN. You never answer. If ghosts don't exist, why do people see them?

SAM. Because we're constantly seeing what isn't there.

(*Gesturing to the patio doors.*) We see the Plough instead of a bunch of stars. The Man in the Moon. The face of Jesus on a slice of toast. If you want ghosts, you'll find them – in the shadows, behind curtains…

LAUREN. Doing pottery with Demi Moore.

(*Off their looks.*) C'mon, he was my first crush!

SAM. But more than anything… you see them because the laws of thermodynamics are really fucking hard to understand. Ghosts are the easy answer. Like, I don't know, blaming Albanians…

JENNY. Sam! Don't be a wanker.

BEN. It's fine. And sometimes the easy answer's right. Feel your radiator.

JENNY (*touches it*). It's warm.

BEN. Your thermostat was switched off.

JENNY. Thank you, Ben!

SAM gives a sardonic nod of thanks.

You realise nothing you say will change my mind?

SAM. Is that a challenge?

JENNY. I know what I heard. And tonight, you'll hear it too.

A sudden shrill cry from Phoebe through the baby monitor makes them all jump.

SAM. I told you kids were creepy.

Phoebe cries again. SAM *makes to go upstairs but* JENNY *beats him to it, exiting.*

LAUREN *pours herself the last of the bottle of wine.*

LAUREN. We need more wine!! If we're about to disprove the laws of physics, then my professional psychiatric evaluation is that we all need to get shit-faced.

SAM. The off-licence will be shut.

JENNY*'s voice can be heard soothing Phoebe through the monitor.*

JENNY (*offstage*). It's alright, darling.

SAM (*realising* LAUREN*'s drunk a lot*). Maybe we should call it a night. Ask the ghost to reschedule.

JENNY (*offstage, lifting Phoebe out of her cot*). Come on, baba… / Sssh, sssh…

BEN. I know a place round the corner.

SAM. A Cockney speakeasy?

The baby monitor cuts out suddenly –

BEN. A corner shop – sells halal meat and twenty-four-hour booze.

LAUREN *looks hopefully at* SAM.

SAM (*sighs reluctantly*). Alright… What do you fancy? Red? White? Beer? 'Spirits'?

LAUREN. All of them. And, boys… Play nicely.

SAM. I'll be gentle.

(*Exiting to hall.*) Come on, mate! You can tell me more about your past lives…

BEN *makes a resigned face to* LAUREN – *she smiles back. He exits.*

(*Offstage.*) Look out: guillotine!

The front door closes.

The baby monitor comes back on – Phoebe murmuring in her sleep.

LAUREN *gets up, holding her wine glass, and goes to look out of the patio doors.*

The security light springs on suddenly, startling her. There's nothing out there.

JENNY (*offstage*). Sssh. Sssh. I love you, baby.

(*Kisses her.*) Sleep well.

The light goes out. LAUREN*'s moves away from the cold emptiness of the garden, her attention drawn to the photos of Phoebe on the bookcase. She drains the last of her wine, staring at them.*

Through the monitor, we hear the bedroom door close and JENNY *coming back downstairs.* LAUREN *moves quickly away from the photos as* JENNY *enters, surprised to find* SAM *and* BEN *gone.*

LAUREN. They went to get wine.

JENNY *crosses to check the monitor.* LAUREN *sets her empty glass on the counter.*

Sam's a sarcastic bastard, huh?

JENNY. But we laugh along.

LAUREN. Oh sure, he's a hoot. Until you're the target.

JENNY *puts clingfilm over the risotto.*

JENNY. How about a coffee?

LAUREN. Caffeine sounds good.

LAUREN sits.

JENNY. I moved her into our room.

She puts the risotto in the fridge.

I suppose you think I'm crazy too.

She puts the kettle on.

LAUREN. I work in mental health. I think everyone's crazy.

(*Then.*) You're frightened. I can see that.

JENNY gets the cafetière out and starts to put coffee in.

JENNY. I've been scared before, obviously. But like normal
scared. You know, dodgy minicabs. Bungee-jumping. Or God.
I was bloody terrified of God. I thought he could read my
mind...

LAUREN laughs.

...work out when I was thinking about boys... But this was
different, Lauren. When I heard it – him – crying... I
screamed. And, shit... don't tell Sam... I realised I was damp.
I was so scared, I'd wet myself.

(*Embarrassed, regretting confiding.*) I mean, having a baby
doesn't help your bladder control, but still... so stupid.

She takes the milk out of the fridge.

LAUREN. No...

JENNY. The police thought I was nuts. I'm dreading them
calling back.

She takes mugs from the cupboard.

LAUREN. It's not stupid. Fear is what's kept humans alive for
millions of years. It's the strongest of all emotions. Stronger
than love.

JENNY. Really?

LAUREN. I think most of us, if we were scared enough, would run off, leave our loved ones to be eaten.

JENNY. That isn't true. I'd never leave Phoebe.

This hangs in the air for a moment. The kettle clicks off.

LAUREN. When I was young, my parents would drive us out to visit these ghost towns that'd been left behind after the gold rush. Old wooden houses and saloon bars, exactly like they were when the gold ran out.

JENNY *pours the water into the cafetière.*

My brother and I used to run around the shacks, chatting to phantom forty-niners. As a kid, I just assumed ghosts were real.

JENNY. But have you ever seen one?

Beat.

LAUREN. Something happened to me once… that didn't make sense.

JENNY. Go on…

LAUREN. I was thirteen, and there was a girl in my class. Ida. I loved her… I was probably a bit 'in love' with her. She had this awesome shock of red hair that defied gravity. And she was so beautiful, and clever. We'd sit in her bedroom, listen to Nirvana.

JENNY. / Course!

She starts to plunge the cafetière.

LAUREN. We'd chat for hours. And she kept parakeets.

JENNY. Really?

LAUREN. They'd fly round her room, and she was training them to talk.

JENNY *laughs.*

She was kooky. We lived in this small, dull jock-town and she was the only person I felt understood me. But she was unhappy. She didn't like her stepdad. She wanted to find her biological father. He lived somewhere in Arizona. And then, one Saturday, I came home from the mall, and my parents told me that Ida was dead.

JENNY. Bloody hell.

LAUREN. She'd fallen from her bedroom window, onto the street.

JENNY (*shocked*). How?

She pours the coffee.

LAUREN. People thought her stepdad had pushed her, but at the inquest, it came out he wasn't even in the house. She'd been alone.

JENNY. / So...?

LAUREN. The most likely theory was one of her parakeets had flown out the window and Ida had tried to catch it. I was heartbroken.

JENNY. And afterwards, you saw her again?

She hands LAUREN *a coffee.*

LAUREN. No... that I'd have understood. But it was before I heard.

(*Off* JENNY*'s confused look.*) That afternoon. I saw her at the mall. She was in one of the glass elevators, going up, her hair like this beautiful explosion, and she smiled and waved to me. Only she died in the morning. She must have been dead for hours by then.

JENNY. Have you told many people?

LAUREN. Just one other. It seemed too crazy, you know?

JENNY. Yes! Except it was the opposite. I thought I'd go mad if I didn't tell anyone.

LAUREN. But maybe you don't have to be afraid. For years after Ida died – at night, I'd hear parakeets...

JENNY. That's creepy.

LAUREN. No. I found it comforting. Ghosts... fill the gaps. Your Margaret – maybe that table and the tools aren't the only thing she left behind.

JENNY (*hardly daring to say it out loud*). Frank...?

The word is swallowed by the mating noises of foxes outside.
The security light comes on.

LAUREN. The unholy sounds of bestial sex.

JENNY crosses to the sofa, taking the cafetière with her.

JENNY. Ben seems nice.

LAUREN. Oh, was that a – 'speaking of bestial sex'?

JENNY. No! I just meant... he's a... / good guy.

LAUREN. Sam hates him.

JENNY. Sam has ridiculously high standards.

LAUREN. That why he married you?

JENNY. I didn't / mean...

LAUREN. I'm kidding. Ben's... good enough.

She sips her coffee.

I just got tired of scrolling through the endless stream of other
people's happiness.

JENNY. Thank you for staying.

LAUREN. I have an ulterior motive. I've known Sam twenty
years and I've never once seen him proved wrong. Tonight
could be historic. Don't fail me!

JENNY (*laughs*). I used to love it. The way he was always so...

LAUREN. Smug?

JENNY. Certain. Like a walking Wikipedia.

LAUREN laughs.

When we first met in that refugee camp. Our year of doing
good –

LAUREN. Uganda?

JENNY. Yeah. We'd spend the day helping these poor people,
and then at night, we'd go and lie on a big hill, looking up at
the stars, and Sam explained the whole bloody universe to me.

LAUREN. 'Astronomy for Idiots'?

JENNY. I was his idiot.

She stands by the patio doors, holding her coffee, looking at the night sky.

He had these stories about the constellations –

LAUREN. His star-nerd chat-up lines.

JENNY. My favourite was about two Chinese lovers – a weaver girl and a cowherd – who were banished to opposite sides of the Silver River, but, once a year, a flock of magpies would form a bridge so they could meet up.

LAUREN. Cute.

JENNY. He showed me how the Silver River was the Milky Way, and there were these two stars on either side. The Lovers.

LAUREN. He make you hold his telescope?

JENNY. It wasn't like that! We'd lie there for hours. He'd talk and I'd listen. I know that sounds pathetic, but I loved it. I felt like a sponge, soaking it all up. Astronomy, history, politics, art… as if everything humans had done was a star map, and if you could join the dots, you'd see the whole picture. And then, one night, I looked up at the sky and realised something. I didn't believe in God any more. Sam had explained Him away.

LAUREN. What did you do?

JENNY. Phoned my mum. She cried.

LAUREN smiles.

But I knew Sam was right.

LAUREN. You believed in him instead.

JENNY. Maybe.

(*A sad beat.*) But it goes both ways, right? I need him to believe in me.

Through the monitor, Phoebe starts to cry, soft at first.
JENNY gets up.

There's something here, Lauren.

(*Heads to the door.*) And I'm sorry, but I don't think it's like your parakeets.

Phoebe's cry intensifies.

It's not comforting.

She exits. LAUREN *sits for a beat, sipping her coffee, listening to Phoebe's cry. Then we hear the front door open.*

SAM (*offstage*). Voilá! The booze-hunters return!

Through the monitor JENNY *soothes Phoebe.*

JENNY (*offstage*). It's okay, darling…

Phoebe calms. SAM *and* BEN *enter,* BEN *holding two bags of bottles, like* SAM's *long-suffering Sherpa.*

SAM. Stick them there, mate.

BEN *puts the bags on the counter and starts unpacking them.*

We have a cheeky little Cab Sav. Couple of Merlots. A little Pinot Grig…

BEN. And Jack Daniel's.

He plonks it on the counter.

SAM. Where's Jen?

Phoebe whimpers.

JENNY (*offstage*). It's okay…

SAM. Ah. I'll stick my head in.

He crosses to the door.

LAUREN (*pointedly*). They're in your bedroom.

SAM *registers this, annoyed, and goes upstairs.* LAUREN *crosses to the kitchen.* BEN *is opening a bottle of wine.*

(*Quietly.*) How was it?

BEN. Fine. Till we had to pay. I look round and he's standing outside, waiting.

Through the monitor, we hear SAM *enter the bedroom.*

SAM (*offstage*). What's she doing / in here?

JENNY (*offstage*). Ssh!

LAUREN. I'll give you money.

BEN. Wouldn't have minded except he chose / it all.

SAM (*offstage*). Jen, put her in her / cot.

JENNY (*offstage*). No!

(*To Phoebe.*) It's / okay, Phoebs...

BEN (*anger creeping in*). You should have seen him. Showing off. In a corner shop!

SAM (*offstage*). Jen...

BEN (*mimicking* SAM). 'Oh no, Ben, I think we'll go for something a little more "robust". Maybe a cheeky little South African number, mate.'

SAM (*offstage*). Jen!

BEN. Something about the way people like him say 'mate' – like they're on a fucking safari, trying to fit in with the natives.

SAM (*offstage, forcefully*). Take her back to her room.

LAUREN (*a warning*). Sam is one of my oldest friends.

She holds out her wine glass.

JENNY (*offstage*). Give me one good reason.

BEN. Right.

He pours wine into her glass.

SAM (*offstage*). She could roll out of our / bed!

JENNY (*offstage*). Oh, now you're / worried.

BEN. And maybe a bit more than that? Back in the day?

SAM (*offstage*). Just do it, Jenny!

JENNY (*offstage*). For Christ's sake!

The monitor cuts out.

LAUREN. No.

BEN. Much to your disappointment.

LAUREN. Fuck you.

She takes a swig. BEN *smiles – he puts his arms around her lustfully.*

BEN. Sorry, I forgot – getting into people's heads – that's your job. I'm just good with my hands.

He runs his hands down her body, as the monitor comes back on.

SAM (*offstage, to Phoebe*). Sssh! You're back, baby.

JENNY (*offstage*). Arsehole.

LAUREN *reacts to* BEN*'s touch, moulding her body towards his.*

SAM (*offstage*). You can't keep moving / her around –

JENNY (*offstage*). This room is / not safe!

SAM (*offstage*). It's fine.

(*Soothing to Phoebe.*) Night night, baba…

Beat.

BEN. Wish she was yours?

SAM (*offstage*). Mummy and Daddy love you.

BEN (*leans in, whispered*). 'Should have married me, Sammy, I think you'll find.'

Beat. We hear SAM *and* JENNY *walking downstairs, then* LAUREN *slaps* BEN *hard, surprising them both.*

SAM *and* JENNY *enter, registering the tension.*

SAM. Alright, Loz?

LAUREN (*concealing her upset*). Of course. I just need the bathroom.

She crosses to the toilet.

JENNY. God, I need a drink.

BEN *pours her a glass.*

SAM (*protective of* LAUREN). Okay, mate?

BEN (*tetchily*). Yes, 'mate'.

LAUREN *gives a short scream from the toilet, making them all jump.*

Lauren?

He's on his way across the room as LAUREN *pushes the toilet door open, looking embarrassed.*

LAUREN. Sorry… I'm a dumbass.

JENNY. What happened?

LAUREN *holds up Phoebe's teddy bear.*

LAUREN. This was in the sink, in a pool of water.

JENNY. / Mister Bear!

LAUREN. It just gave me a shock.

SAM. How did it get / in there?

BEN (*sniffs*). That's not water. Smell. / White spirit.

JENNY (*shocked*). White spirit.

LAUREN. / Jesus.

BEN. The sink's full of it.

SAM (*to* JENNY). Did you do that?

JENNY (*angrily*). What do you think?

LAUREN. Ben?

BEN. Course bloody not! I haven't been in there since before dinner!

SAM (*beat; then*). You went to get toilet paper, when Loz spilt my / wine.

BEN. Oh, for five seconds!

JENNY. Stop it!!

　(*Then.*) Who was the last one in? Was it me?

LAUREN (*realising, thrown*). No, me. I flushed the toilet paper, after we'd mopped up.

SAM. Was the sink empty?

LAUREN (*thinks*). Yes. I… I washed my hands. It was empty.

BEN. And no one's been in since?

　They look from one to another.

JENNY (*re: bear*). Sam! How did he get in there?

SAM. I don't know. Where was it?

JENNY. I… I put it on that shelf. When I was tidying.

SAM. / Are you sure?

JENNY (*to* LAUREN). Didn't I?

LAUREN. I think / so…

JENNY. And I put the white spirit in here.

　She goes into the toilet.

　On top of the cupboard. It's still / here!

SAM. The bottle must have leaked.

JENNY. The safety cap's on.

SAM. Maybe there's a / crack…

JENNY. No, Sam! This is impossible!

BEN. It's a poltergeist.

SAM. Oh, for crying out loud! Stop! It's not impossible. / It's just… odd.

JENNY. How does a teddy bear move itself?

SAM. It doesn't. You must / have forgotten…

JENNY. Did anyone touch it?

BEN *and* LAUREN *shake their heads.*

SAM. / Okay let's just…

JENNY. Jesus! What if this had been daytime? If Phoebe found it?

SAM. Jenny, she's barely crawling on the / floor!

JENNY. But it's her toy! It's horrible, Sam! This is poisonous!

She pulls the plug out of the sink, shaken, panicky.

SAM (*soothing*). There will be a very simple reason.

(*Tries to touch her.*) I'll work it / out.

JENNY (*moves away*). How? I put it there!! (*Points to the shelf.*) None of us moved it. So who / did?

SAM. Jen, trust me.

JENNY. No! I can't any more.

(*Holding the bear out.*) This feels like… a warning.

SAM. / Come on!

JENNY. A threat.

(*Suddenly connecting it.*) Like the window in her room.

SAM. / Jenny!

JENNY. Whatever this thing is, it's not / just in the bedroom any more…

SAM. There isn't a thing!

JENNY. It's getting closer…

A bloodcurdling screech from the garden. The security light springs on. They all jump – their 'fight or flight' instinct engaged.

BEN. / Shit!

LAUREN. Fuck!

SAM (*realising before the others*). It's foxes!

(*Rattled despite himself.*) Jesus, look at you all! There will be an explanation.

BEN. Yeah? Go on… mate.

They all look to SAM. *For the first time, put on the spot, he is unsure…*

SAM. Things cannot appear and disappear.

JENNY. You're wrong, Sam. This is it. He's coming.

Lights down, as the foxes scream again.

End of Act One.

Interval.

ACT TWO

Scene Four

*The time on the clock is now 00:05. It's started raining outside.
The weather worsens through the scene.*

*The white spirit and Mister Bear are on the coffee table –
newspaper under them – next to the baby monitor.* SAM, JENNY
and LAUREN *sit tensely, staring at them.*

JENNY. So?

SAM (*tetchily*). I'm still thinking.

> LAUREN *photographs the bear and bottle with her phone.*

What are you doing?

LAUREN. Putting it on Facebook.

SAM. Oh God! We'll be a laughing / stock!

JENNY. I'd rather you didn't. In case anyone from work saw.

SAM. Help! Our child's teacher is being haunted by a petroleum-
based spirit!

> *There's a thumping on the glass of the patio doors. They all
> jump, as the security light comes on, they see* BEN, *illuminated.*

LAUREN. Jesus! Ben.

> *She goes to open the doors and* BEN *steps in, shaking off the
> rain.*

BEN. Sorry. Filthy habit.

JENNY. I can't take this. I feel like I need the loo, but I don't
want to go in there.

BEN. This is what it's like on a vigil. You've got to be ready for
anything. I was at this haunted pub once, in Essex. We waited
hours, nothing happening, and then a pint glass flew across
the room.

SAM. Average night out in Essex.

> BEN *brings the Jack Daniel's bottle and some mugs over to the sofa.*

BEN. Ghost-hunting essential. Dutch courage.

> (*Re: mugs.*) I couldn't find glasses.

> *He pours whiskey into the mugs and hands one to* JENNY.

> This'll get you to 2:22.

LAUREN. Let's play a drinking game!

> (*Off their reluctant looks.*) Oh, come on! Like the old days, Sam, in your bedsit. Truth or Dare!

SAM. No. A quiz.

> LAUREN *groans.*

> If you can answer my questions, I drink. If you can't, you drink.

LAUREN. Okay!

SAM. Alexa, dim the living-room lights.

> *Alexa doesn't respond. The others laugh.*

> Bloody hell! What have you done to her?

JENNY. She's showing female solidarity. Alexa, please dim the dining-room lights.

ALEXA. Okay.

> *The lights dim.*

SAM. Perfect!

> (*Theatrically.*) It's time to play – 'Do Ghosts Exist?'

> *He hums a dramatic quiz theme to build tension.*

BEN. Jesus.

JENNY. Try living with it.

SAM. Fingers on buzzers! Question one... If ghosts exist, why aren't there absolutely loads of them?

JENNY. How do you mean?

SAM. Why aren't they flooding into our world in their thousands? Like refugees, desperate to escape? Seriously – there's a portal to Earth that will let you see your family again? You'd be straight in there.

LAUREN. God, yeah! I'd be showing off, walking through walls, / spraying ectoplasm...

JENNY. Maybe it's not easy to travel. Like for refugees. It's a difficult journey and only a few make it.

SAM considers this.

SAM. Good answer.

LAUREN holds SAM's mug to his lips, forcing him to drink.

BEN. That was easy.

He refills SAM's mug.

JENNY. Question two?

SAM. Geography. The most popular locations to see ghosts are...

LAUREN. / Castles.

BEN. Monasteries.

LAUREN. Stately homes.

JENNY. That's just the famous ghosts. I bet most appear in ordinary houses.

SAM. Agreed. The vast majority of sightings are in a domestic situation. Stately, monastic or otherwise.

BEN. So?

SAM. How many people die in their house? Think about your family – your grandparents, aunties, uncles... parents. Where did they take their last breath?

LAUREN (*seeing what he's getting at*). A hospital.

SAM. It's not where we see ghosts, it's where we don't see them. If they really haunt the scene of their death...

LAUREN. They'd all be hanging round hospitals.

SAM. You'd go into an oncology ward and not be able to move for spooks. All the poor bastards who died of lung cancer, breast cancer... Where are they?

Beat.

JENNY (*conceding the point*). One-all.

She drinks, followed by LAUREN *and a reluctant* BEN. LAUREN *refills their mugs.*

LAUREN. Question three?

SAM. Why aren't ghosts naked?

They laugh.

I'm serious. Clothes don't die.

BEN. Do we know that?

SAM. Yes.

LAUREN. Nudist ghosts. That's enough for me.

She goes to drink.

JENNY. Wait. You're confusing ghosts and zombies.

SAM. Not a sentence I thought I'd hear...

JENNY. Ghosts aren't literally dead people walking around. I think they're more like... Facebook.

SAM (*sceptically*). / Right...

JENNY. Every day, Facebook offers you memories. 'This is you seven years ago, falling out of a taxi in Ibiza'... You mostly ignore them, but, every so often one sticks out, cos it sets off some emotional response. A birth, a death, a... funny hat. So you share it again. Maybe ghosts are the universe doing that. Certain people get chosen –

LAUREN. From the scrolling feed of death?

JENNY. Yes! Because something really big or awful happened to them. Or maybe the universe just thinks they deserve a second chance. But physical objects, clothes, that's irrelevant. We're talking about emotion – love, hate, regret – a memory come to life.

LAUREN. I prefer that one.

SAM. Me too. Love it. But it's nonsense. You can't see a memory.

JENNY. Can't you?

(*Crosses to the patio doors*.) What about the stars? You told me once it takes so long for their light to reach us that what we see is how they were in the past. Look through your telescope and find a hundred billion ghosts.

LAUREN *and* BEN (*chanting*). Drink! Drink! Drink! Drink!

SAM (*laughs, acquiescing with a sigh*). Fine!

JENNY *holds* SAM'*s mug to his lips, forcing him to drink*.

BEN. Two-one to Team Believe.

LAUREN *tops up* SAM'*s mug*.

JENNY. Next!

SAM. Question four. This is a big one. Communication. Let's go back to that 'portal from the afterlife' theory, and say – whatever ghosts are – the reason we're not overrun is that the gateway between life and death is a secret only some spirits are in on.

LAUREN. Like the wardrobe to Narnia.

SAM. Precisely!

JENNY. Or, it's known about but dangerous.

BEN. Like running across Sniper's Alley. Not everyone gets through.

SAM. I buy all that. So you're dead, you discover the portal, and it's a really arduous journey; the spectral equivalent of clinging to a dinghy across the freezing sea. You risk your place in eternity, your afterlife, to see your family one last time… Because you want to tell them…?

JENNY. You love them.

BEN. Things are going to be okay.

LAUREN. Where the money's buried.

SAM. Great. It's fucking important, right? And the words you choose, to convey this vital message to people you care about more than anything else in the world?

(*Beat, then he springs up suddenly, loudly.*) Wooooooooooooh!

They jump. LAUREN *laughs, loud and long.*

JENNY. / Bastard.

She turns the main lights back on.

BEN. Not funny.

LAUREN. But he's right. Why wait till the dead of night? Wake your family up and scare the crap out of them?

SAM. Thank you, Loz! Or playing games, like: 'Ooh, I'll let them know I'm okay by making that picture fall off the wall.' Or, the one that always gets me: 'There's a psychic, and my grieving wife's in the audience. To make this interesting, I'll only give him the first letter of my name.'

LAUREN. Why are ghosts so dumb?

SAM. Dumb, inefficient, unnecessarily cruel. Just so... un-human. We're obsessed with communication. It's all we do. Non-stop. Thousands of years honing it till we can send millions of words with the click of a button, and we just forget all that?

Beat.

You know what I might actually believe? An email from the dead. Or a WhatsApp message. It would at least feel... realistic.

LAUREN. Tinder from the dead. Swipe right to meet your doom! I've had dates like that! Cheers!

(*Downs her drink.*) / Two-all.

JENNY. What if they're damaged?

SAM. Pardon?

JENNY. Like somebody with dementia. A ghost is a fragment of a person. Confused. Scared. The picture falling is to get attention. The more we ignore them, the more desperate they become. Question number five –

LAUREN (*topping up her whiskey*). The tiebreaker!

JENNY. What happened to Mister Bear? You never did explain.

All eyes are on SAM.

SAM. Like I said, it must have got put in the toilet when you were tidying. And then, it just fell in the sink.

BEN. What about the white spirit?

SAM. Hundreds of possibilities. A hairline crack in the bottle. It slowly trickled out.

They're not buying this.

Or perhaps some strange anomaly with our plumbing. Some white spirit actually came up out of / the sink...

JENNY. You don't have a clue!

SAM. I'm being logical. Once you eliminate the / impossible –

JENNY. There is something... targeting our daughter, targeting her things, and you think it's some clever academic puzzle!

SAM. / No, I...

JENNY (*decisively, crossing to the door*). I'm moving her back to our room...

SAM (*stepping in her way, gently*). Sweetie! You're tired.

He puts his hands on her arms. She flinches at his touch.

You haven't slept all week. You've inhaled a lot of paint fumes. Trust the quiz. Ghosts do not exist.

BEN. You're wrong. And I have proof.

He stands dramatically.

SAM. Don't tell me? You are a ghost?

BEN. No, but I've lived with one.

SAM. Is that the time? Cab?

BEN. When I was three.

LAUREN. You know imaginary friends don't count?

BEN. It's not funny, Lauren. I had to have an exorcism.

(*Off their shock*.) Yeah, alright, I wasn't gonna tell you.
I thought you might not take me seriously.

SAM *raises his eyebrows to imply it's a bit late for that…*

(*To* JENNY.) This is why I believe you.

JENNY. What happened?

BEN. If I say, is he going to give it 'all that'? Piss on my chips?

JENNY *shoots* SAM *a look*.

SAM. Your pomme frites shall remain un-urinated upon. For now.

He sits, relinquishing the floor.

BEN. Alright.

Beat, BEN *making sure he has their attention…*

I told you I grew up round here. One of the houses we rented
was on Milton Road, down by the waterworks, you know?
Near the marshes.

SAM. Nice area.

BEN. Now. It was rough back then. Mid-seventies. And there'd
been a murder in one of the houses. Not the Krays, but
someone who knew them. They'd stabbed this bloke and he'd
bled out over the floor. Dripped through the ceiling, into the
living room, like it was raining indoors, big red drops. And
however many times they cleaned it, the bloodstain would
always come back.

JENNY. This was your house?

BEN. No, another one. But, you know, it was that kind of street.
Always dark. Even during the day.

SAM. I think this is what's called 'atmosphere'.

BEN. We lived at Number 27. We moved there when I was three
and my sister was two. We were Irish twins. Eleven months
apart. That's her now – Beverley.

He shows them a picture on his phone.

SAM. Nice tattoos.

LAUREN (*she's had enough of* SAM). Will you shut the fuck up?

SAM. I was / just…

LAUREN. Being a condescending prick.

A shocked beat. SAM *is genuinely chastened –*

SAM. Loz, as ever, has the correct diagnosis.

(*To* BEN.) Sorry. Go on.

BEN. We'd been there a month when it started. My sister was saying strange things. Stuff she couldn't possibly have known. About Hitler. The Blitz… One time, Bev told Mum we should go down the Underground, hide from the bombs. How the hell would she know that? A two-year-old?

Beat.

And then, one morning, Mum saw something. She went in the kitchen, and there was this little old lady, standing by the window. And the lady said 'Hello', and my mum said hello back, and then she heard one of us call or fall over, and when she turned back, the old lady was gone.

JENNY. Was she scared?

BEN. No. Mum was a member of the spiritualist church down the road. Did seances, so she understood spirits and that. She said the woman seemed friendly. I think if it'd stopped there, it would've been okay. But my sister started saying about how a lady came to visit us in our room after lights out. And I was saying it too – I had to do what the old woman told me – mind my manners…

JENNY. That's / horrible.

BEN. A few days later, Mum was doing the vacuuming and she stuck her head round our door and me and Bev were sitting on my bed, singing a song.

BEN *sings the first four lines of 'In an Old Dutch Garden (By an Old Dutch Mill)'.*

(*Then.*) Know it?

They shake their heads.

What about you, Alexa?

ALEXA. I don't understand the question.

BEN. No? Neither had Mum. But later, she asked my gran, who said it's from the 1940s.

Beat.

Mum said what got her was the way we were singing – little gaps between each line, like we were learning it. And – this sent a shiver right down her spine – without turning round, Bev says, 'Come in, Mummy. The lady doesn't mind.'

Beat, as they take this in.

And Mum thought maybe it wasn't so good, the ghost being alone with us, even if it was friendly.

JENNY. Oh my / God...

BEN. So that's when she called the priest.

LAUREN. I need more wine!

She pours herself another glass.

BEN. My dad was dead against it. Didn't want 'mumbo-jumbo' near us kids. But Mum knew, you've got to act. Cleanse the house.

JENNY. Did it work, getting the priest in?

BEN. I think so. He sprinkled holy water and asked the old lady to leave us alone. But we moved soon after, anyway. Mum and Dad got divorced.

SAM (*interest piqued*). Really?

BEN (*defensive*). Not cos of the ghost! It was just... these things happen, don't they?

JENNY. / Course.

BEN. He was a lorry driver. Met some bird in Scotland.

(*Getting back on track.*) Anyway, the thing that sticks in my head most... Mum said it was like the old lady didn't realise she wasn't living there any more. She thought it was still her home.

JENNY. You were the intruders?

BEN. Yeah. Like Mum'd wandered into her kitchen and she was being polite.

(*Then.*) Doing those vigils in the stately homes – you start to think ghosts are all headless posh people or pregnant medieval nuns. But this was an ordinary old lady – a nobody – wanting to stay in her shitty little house.

Beat as they think about this. JENNY *finds herself staring at the wallpaper.*

JENNY. Layers.

LAUREN. That's the saddest idea of all. To be a ghost and not even realise it.

JENNY. Perhaps there are thousands of them. We talked about refugees, but maybe they're actually like the homeless. All around us, everywhere, and we just ignore them. People sell it as this great comfort – life after death – but what if it's just a horrible realisation you're irrelevant? That would make me want to throw things. Or scare the people living in my house.

SAM *whispers something in* LAUREN'*s ear. She starts to google on her phone.*

BEN. So? You going to pick it apart?

SAM. I can't, can I?

BEN. / Huh?

SAM. It's not your story.

BEN. I / told you...

SAM. You were three. It's second hand from your mum. We'd need to talk to her.

BEN (*sharply*). My mum's dead.

JENNY. I think I'll make some tea.

She crosses to put the kettle on.

BEN (*tetchily*). I'm going to have another fag.

*He opens the patio doors. The security light comes on. It's
raining harder now, and there is a low roll of thunder.*

SAM. Shitty weather.

LAUREN. At least it might keep the foxes away.

BEN *huddles by the house to stay dry. As he lights up, the
security light clicks off.*

SAM (*stands up*). Can you still see the Plough?

BEN (*looks up, disinterested*). Yeah.

SAM. No you can't.

BEN. / Eh?

SAM. It doesn't exist.

BEN. What / do you mean?

SAM. Human beings, we made it up! What you're looking at is
utter meaningless chaos. The universe is a random mess, but
every nanosecond, our brains are frantically searching for
patterns, craving meaning...

(*To* JENNY.) Lightning at your wedding – inclement weather
or the wrath of God?

There's another roll of thunder outside.

Perception is a choice – based on our beliefs, experiences,
fears, desires... The story your brain chooses to tell. We're all
going on a bear hunt, but when you look into his big goggly
eyes, do you see homicidal hunger, or loneliness?

BEN *moves and the security light clicks on again.*

I think your old lady was an old lady. Walking past the
kitchen window as the morning light floods in. Seen by a tired
mum who attends seances and worries about her kids. A wife
who feels her unfaithful husband slipping away and needs a
reason to keep him close.

A tense beat.

BEN. Bullshit. What about me and my sister singing that song?

SAM. You heard it somewhere. Probably from your gran, who, after all, knew the song, which is...?

He looks to LAUREN.

LAUREN (*looking up from her phone*). Glenn Miller. It's on his Greatest Hits.

She plays a short burst of the song on her phone – we recognise the lyrics BEN *sang.*

BEN (*wounded that she's helped*). / But I...

The security light clicks off.

SAM (*with the air of a victor*). And now, if you'll excuse me, I am knackered.

(*Crosses to* JENNY, *en route to door.*) Sorry, but it's been a long day and I think we all know how this is going to end.

He goes to kiss her.

JENNY. Coward.

SAM. Pardon?

JENNY. You know you're outnumbered. Three against one.

SAM. Are we counting Alexa?

He looks to LAUREN. *She looks away.*

JENNY. We believe. And you hate that, don't you?

Beat.

SAM. Yes. I hate that you would be so stupid.

BEN *throws his cigarette butt away and steps in from the dark, spoiling for a fight.*

BEN. My mum knew what she was talking about. I sat with her when she did seances, saw her chatting to the dead. She said I had the gift too.

SAM. Awesome. You can fix boilers and commune with the dead. You win.

He turns to go, but BEN *gets right in his face.*

BEN. What if I had a message for you, 'mate'? Would that scare you?

LAUREN. / Ben...

SAM. No, mate. Loz – let's do lunch / soon.

BEN (*a surprising intensity*). It means something to you.

SAM. What?

BEN. 2:22.

SAM. What are / you talking...?

BEN. You know why it comes at that time.

SAM (*thrown*). Of course I don't.

BEN. Then you will. Soon.

SAM*'s been rattled by* BEN*'s intensity but tries to laugh it off. There's another rumble of thunder outside.*

SAM. Goodnight, all.

He walks to the door.

BEN (*calls after him*). I reckon you're like my old man.

SAM *pauses* –

Mum said he always slept with the light on. Didn't believe in ghosts, but couldn't kip in the dark. Is that you, 'Sammy'? Secretly scared of what's hiding where the light can't reach?

SAM *turns to face him.*

Might be worse than just lizards.

Beat as they hold each other's gaze.

SAM. Sod it. I will stay up. Just to see the look of disappointment on your faces.

Outside we can hear the foxes.

LAUREN. They're back.

She closes the patio door.

We are nowhere near drunk enough for this.

She goes to pour herself another wine as JENNY *brings over the mugs of tea.*

JENNY. It's this house. We never argued before we came here.

SAM. We never argued before we had a kid.

JENNY. Is it our fault? Did we make this happen?

SAM. You're right, we shouldn't have built the extension on that ancient burial ground.

JENNY. Fine...

She goes back into the kitchen to put away the milk.

LAUREN. What do you mean?

JENNY. We've been so... unkind.

SAM. 'Unkind'?

JENNY. To the house. We stripped it. Years and years of love and warmth – people growing up, marrying, fucking, having children and dying. Layer after layer of... I don't know – somebody else's story! And we just pulled it all / out.

SAM. We made it nicer.

JENNY. No.

(*Re: patio doors.*) I hate those doors. They're cold and hard and... wrong.

SAM. We chose them together!

JENNY. You chose them and I listened! I said I didn't like them, and I said I didn't feel right about this house. It's not ours.

SAM. Oh, / please!

JENNY. We're trying to force it to be, but I think...

SAM. What?

JENNY. I think it's reacting against us.

The thunder is getting closer.

SAM. Lauren, can you analyse my wife, please? She appears to have gone nuts.

LAUREN. I don't do friends.

JENNY. We broke our promise! We told Margaret we'd look after it. If she could see it now...

SAM (*'Margaret' voice*). Oh! My poor Frank's wardrobe! You burnt it in the garden!

JENNY. Did you?

Beat.

Did you burn it?

SAM (*shrugs*). Yes. One day, when you were at your mum's. It was ugly.

(*Off her appalled look.*) Oh, come on...

(*Shouts, as if to the house.*) Sorry, Frank!

JENNY. Stop it!

She throws the fruit bowl at him, narrowly missing. It smashes against the wall. The others react with shock.

SAM (*shaken*). Jesus, / Jen...

JENNY (*an unfamiliar edge to her voice*). This is your fault. You promised Margaret.

SAM. / I...

JENNY. You've put our daughter in danger.

SAM (*quiet, shaken*). 'Danger'?

(*Feeling almost like he's talking to a stranger.*) Jenny...

There's a huge clap of thunder, and a flash of lightning, illuminating the garden, making them all jump.

It wakes Phoebe – there's a cry through the baby monitor.

(*Still shaken.*) I'll go...

JENNY. No. I am taking her out of that room now.

She turns to leave. BEN *steps forward.*

BEN. Can I come?

LAUREN *and* SAM *look at him, surprised.*

I could take a look at the bedroom, see if there's anything I can pick up?

JENNY *nods her consent.*

SAM. For God's sake…!

BEN *looks smug as he and* JENNY *exit.*

(*Angrily, as they go.*) Jenny!

The door shuts. SAM *lets out an angry, exasperated sigh. We hear* JENNY *and* BEN *go upstairs, then, through the monitor, the creak of the door as they enter the bedroom.*

JENNY (*offstage*). It's okay, darling.

Phoebe's crying subsides,

Mummy's going to move you. It's okay…

BEN (*offstage*). She's beautiful.

The monitor switches abruptly off.

LAUREN *starts to pick up the broken pieces of fruit bowl from the floor. Outside the rain is heavy.*

SAM (*sulkily*). Whose bloody side are you on?

LAUREN. I'm Switzerland.

SAM *snorts, unamused.* LAUREN *crosses to put the pieces of bowl in the bin.*

SAM. Parrots.

LAUREN (*tensing*). What?

She slides the bowl into the bin, her back to SAM.

SAM. I was going, there's no way Loz will believe this crap. But then I think… Parrots.

LAUREN *turns to face him, taken aback.*

Christ, you were off your face. Trapping me in some poky corner of the student union, going off on one about your beautiful ghost mate and her phantom parrots!

A hurt beat.

LAUREN. They were parakeets.

SAM. God, I didn't have a clue how to respond.

LAUREN. You laughed.

SAM. Sorry. I probably wasn't the only one?

LAUREN. I never told anybody else.

This hangs in the air – a realisation for SAM *it meant a lot more to her than he realised.*

LAUREN *pours herself another glass of wine.*

SAM. You know you can do better than Ben?

LAUREN. Trust me, I tried pretty hard.

She takes a sip, then:

Did you really lose your phone on Sark?

SAM (*thrown by this random question*). Yes. Why would I lie?

LAUREN. Maybe you liked the idea of Jenny sitting here, scared. Needing you.

SAM. I didn't know she was scared. There was no 'ghost' before I left.

LAUREN. I've been half wondering if it's you.

SAM (*shocked*). Pardon?

LAUREN. Whether you're doing this. Leaving windows open. Drowning Mister Bear. Perhaps you never even went to Sark. You just hid here, creeping Jenny out.

SAM. That's completely fucked up!

LAUREN. You love to be in control. I think you'll / find.

SAM. Oh, cut the Freudian bollocks, I'm not / a client...

LAUREN. I watched you through that quiz. Were you even drinking?

SAM looks surprised. LAUREN picks up his whiskey mug.

There's three shots of whiskey in here. You cheat.

SAM shifts uncomfortably.

Is that your master plan? Stay sober, let us get drunk and fight it out?

SAM. Not everyone enjoys drinking as much as you.

LAUREN. Did you go to Sark?

SAM. You're supposed to be my mate, Loz.

She holds his gaze.

Of course I bloody did.

LAUREN. Okay. Sorry. But if that's true, I can only see one possible explanation. …

She picks up Mister Bear.

There is a ghost.

The thunder rumbles as JENNY enters.

JENNY. I've moved her. Ben says –

SAM. You've left him up there by himself?

LAUREN. What does / that mean?

JENNY. He says her room has a feel.

(*Challenging.*) It's what I think.

SAM. Then that's why he said it. It's cosy in the echo chamber.

JENNY crosses to the kitchen and opens a cupboard.

What are you doing?

She pulls out the envelope with the crucifix her mum sent.

JENNY. Putting the crucifix up.

She takes it out of the envelope.

SAM. This was his idea?

JENNY. No, mine. I'm getting Frank's hammer.

SAM. Jenny!

She opens the patio door and walks down towards the shed. The security light clicks on. The storm is intense now, rain lashing down.

This is getting out of hand! Come in! Let's talk about this!

JENNY (*from the garden*). Nothing to talk about. I'm looking after my child.

SAM. Our child!

JENNY *marches back towards the house, holding a hammer and the crucifix. She's soaked.*

SAM *stands in the doorway.*

Give it to me.

JENNY. No.

SAM. This is insane! What's it going to do? Ward off evil? Chase away demons?

JENNY. Get out of my way.

SAM. No!

She moves to go past. SAM tries to grab the crucifix. She dodges and bangs into the patio door, hurting her knee.

JENNY. Ow! Fucking hell!! I hate those fucking doors!!

She drops the hammer and crucifix on the floor and sits on the sofa, nursing her knee.

SAM (*goes to put a hand on her*). You okay?

JENNY. Get away from me!

We hear the foxes outside.

SAM *sits on the opposite side of the sofa.* LAUREN *lurks in the kitchen, drinking, making herself scarce.*

SAM. What's happening to us, Jenny? What do we / do here?

JENNY. We should think about selling the house.

SAM lets out a moan.

SAM. Do you realise how much money we'd lose? The stamp / duty alone...

JENNY. Is that the most important thing?

SAM. No!

(*Then.*) This is meant to be our home. For... / ever.

JENNY. We could stay with my parents whilst the sale / goes through.

SAM. Oh, they'd love that. Get you back into the fold.

JENNY stands and picks up the crucifix.

Do you miss it? Believing? Is that what this is all about?

JENNY. I need to think about Phoebe. I need to protect her.

SAM. The only thing she needs protecting from is you.

A shocked beat.

I didn't mean that. I'm sorry...

JENNY picks up the hammer. For a moment it looks as if she will hit him.

(*Scared.*) Jen...!

She exits – huge emotional damage has been done.

Fuck!

He sinks into the sofa, a picture of despair.

LAUREN. Would it kill you to compromise? Say to her, okay, maybe you did hear something.

SAM. It's a slippery slope, Loz. Believe in ghosts, and what next? The Earth is flat, there's no climate change. Jews run the / world!

LAUREN. Oh, please...

SAM. It all comes from the same place. The beauty of a simple answer to a complicated question. Screw the 'experts', we want to believe.

LAUREN. This is your wife.

SAM. That's why I care! Before I met her she was miserable. You should see her parents' house. Jesus staring down from every wall, like some sort of Messianic CCTV. I saved her from that.

From upstairs, we hear the distant thud of the crucifix being nailed to the wall.

It's lizards versus monkeys, Loz. Choose your side.

LAUREN. I worry about you, Sammy. Understanding how gravity works doesn't stop you falling. Or make it hurt less when you land.

We hear BEN *come down the stairs. He enters, holding the hammer.*

BEN. All done.

LAUREN *has drained her wine. She's definitely drunk now.*

LAUREN. I'm going to brave the haunted bathroom.

She exits to the toilet – a little unsteady.

BEN. I've got to compliment you on this place. Your taste. Your vision. Hardly a trace of how it looked before. That's what you do, though, isn't it? Your lot.

SAM. Pardon?

BEN. You come in, take these old houses and wipe them clean. With your expensive doors and your cheap Albanians. Sneering at the people who used to live here. Ramping up the prices, forcing us out.

SAM. It's called progress.

BEN. I sold my mum's house to a couple like you. Listened to them walking around, laughing at her furniture, her carpets, her pictures of the Queen. Boasting how they were going to 'knock that through' and 'pull that out'. Like vampires eyeing a vein. And what did I do?

(*With self-disgust.*) Gave them my fucking business card.

(*Then.*) I spend my whole life working for people like you, tearing houses apart to get rid of any sign of people like me. And you all think you're so original, but you know what? They all look the same. They look like you. Smug and fragile. Cos underneath the IKEA kitchen, and the polished floorboards... we're still here.

The baby monitor comes back on.

If I was Frank, I'd haunt you.

There's a thunder clap outside.

SAM. Lauren always had terrible taste in men.

BEN (*pointedly*). I know.

From the toilet, we hear LAUREN *vomit.*

BEN *puts the hammer down and crosses to the toilet, pushing the door open.*

LAUREN. I got sick.

BEN (*sighs*). Wipe your mouth.

He tears off some toilet paper.

Here –

She wipes her face and throws the paper into the toilet. We hear JENNY *coming downstairs.*

LAUREN. Perhaps we should go.

BEN. And miss all the fun?

JENNY *enters.*

JENNY. She's back in her room.

SAM. Good.

JENNY. And the crucifix is over her cot.

SAM. Jenny, listen...

JENNY. I've listened enough.

SAM. I've tried to explain...

JENNY. Oh you have. Living with you is one long lecture.

(To the others.) He even explained childbirth to me. I'm there pushing Phoebe out my clacker and he's critiquing my sodding technique.

(To SAM.) Well, you know what, I'm not one of your students. Or your 'idiots'… So I don't want any more explanations. I want to do something.

(Turns to BEN.) I'm ready.

BEN. We're going to try and make contact.

SAM. With what?

BEN. Whatever's in this house.

JENNY. Ben thinks he knows how. Ways he learnt from his mum.

BEN. Thought it might be a comfort. To know if / Phoebe's safe.

SAM. This has gone far enough! He is not staying in my house! Sorry, Lauren – Alexa, book an Uber.

Alexa does not respond.

(A roar of frustrated rage.) Arrgh! Book a fucking Uber, for crying out loud!

(Still nothing – turns to JENNY.) You've turned her against me!

JENNY. Who's irrational / now?

SAM *(to* BEN). You need to stay away from my wife!

(Then.) Where's my fucking phone?

LAUREN. You lost it, / right?

SAM. Jesus! I'm walking to the / cab office!

JENNY. I see it now. Ben's right. You're scared. All of it – the facts, the scientific theories – it's a wall. I thought it was just there to shut me up. But actually, it's to protect you, from your biggest nightmare – a world where everything can't be explained.

SAM. I… Well…

Thunder outside. SAM *falters, for once speechless.*

BEN. Hands up for speaking to the spirits.

BEN and JENNY *put their hands up.*

SAM (*cornered, a note of desperation*). Loz?

LAUREN. Who put Mister Bear in that sink, Sam?

SAM has no answer.

How did the white spirit get in there?

Beat.

SAM (*hating to have to say it*). I don't know!

LAUREN puts her hand up. SAM*'s shoulders slump, beaten.*

BEN. Let's reach out.

Thunder and lightning, loud and shocking, then snap to black.

Scene Five

The clock races forwards to 01:15. It's still raining outside.

The room is in darkness – just the flickering lights of the baby monitor on the coffee table.

BEN *strikes his lighter. He's standing by the dining table.* LAUREN *and* JENNY *sit either side of the table.* SAM *is on the sofa, shrouded in darkness, despondent.*

The table is now bare apart from some candles. BEN *starts to light them.*

BEN. We need a circle of light.

He places the candles on surfaces around the room, forming a ring around the table.

LAUREN (*enjoying the theatre of it*). This is so... Victorian. You can imagine them, can't you? Sitting in their parlour, summoning the other side.

BEN. This could get weird.

JENNY. Is it safe?

BEN. My mum always did it like this.

He places the last candle then sits centrally at the table.

It's fine. If you follow my instructions.

(*Aimed at* SAM.) Everyone.

They look at SAM.

SAM (*mutters to himself*). Fuck's sake...

He crosses to join them at the table, sulkily.

BEN. Switch off your phones. We need total focus.

We see the light of JENNY *and* LAUREN*'s phones as they switch them off.*

Right. In the name of God and Jesus / Christ...

SAM. I thought you weren't religious?

BEN. Better safe than sorry.

(*Continuing*.) ...Protect us from evil. Let us communicate only with powers and entities of the light. And if there are entities of darkness, let us be strong enough to overcome them. Amen.

LAUREN (*getting spooked*). Shit got real.

BEN. The spirit we want to contact is...

JENNY. Frank.

SAM. I can't believe we're doing this.

BEN. We know Frank has a connection with this table, so please, can you all put your hands on it?

LAUREN *and* JENNY *obey. They wait for* SAM. *He gives a despairing sigh and reluctantly complies.*

He's going to use it to communicate. Understand this – it may move.

SAM. Jenny...

BEN. Silence.

(*A deep breath, focusing.*) Frank, are you there?

A tense beat, then a mobile phone pings with an annoying text alert.

Bollocks!

(*Turns it off.*) Sorry about that.

He takes another deep breath, refocusing.

Frank, we hope, when you're ready, you'll come into the light.

A long beat. There's a whimper from the baby monitor, but nothing else.

Remember, guys, we don't move the table. He does. Frank, if you're here, please join us. Give us a sign.

A really long tense beat as they wait, then SAM *stands suddenly, shocking them.*

SAM. Sorry, there's only so much bullshit I can swallow in one sitting. Lauren, hope to see you soon. Ben, we've got your / card.

JENNY. Sit / down.

SAM. You don't need me for this / circus.

JENNY. If you want me and Phoebe to still be here when you wake up, sit down.

Beat. SAM *sits, chastened.*

BEN. Let's try again.

They put their hands back on the table.

Deep breaths. In. Out. In. Out. You're sending positive energy into the table.

Frank, we're focusing all our powers now, fella, asking you to join us. If you're here, buddy, give us a sign.

A long, focused beat. Then another whimper from the monitor distracts them.

Suddenly, the table moves, just slightly.

JENNY. Oh God! Did you feel that?

LAUREN. That was weird.

BEN. Thank you, spirit. Are we talking to Frank?

The table moves again, more definitely this time. They all flinch, even SAM.

You lived in this house? With Margaret?

The table moves.

LAUREN. Shit, / shit!

JENNY. It's working!

BEN. I told / you!

SAM. Oh, for God's sake!

(Stands, re: BEN.*)* It's him! He's doing it! You're right, Lauren, it's exactly like Victorian times.

Beat, all eyes scrutinise BEN.

BEN. Fine. I'll take my hands off.

He does this, leaving LAUREN *and* JENNY *touching the table.* SAM *stands, arms folded, a model of cynicism.*

BEN. Frank, are you still there? Focus, girls. Keep your hands still and let him in.

A long intense beat. It seems nothing will happen. SAM *looks triumphant, but, then, the table moves again.* JENNY *gasps.*

God bless you, Frank!

JENNY. We're not doing anything!

SAM. Jenny, this isn't / real.

JENNY. But you saw it!

SAM. Yes, it moved.

BEN. He admits / it!

SAM. But there's an explanation.

(Realising they're going to hate this.) A scientific explanation.

BEN. Of course there is! Well, go on, Albert fucking Einstein.

SAM. It's called the ideomotor effect. Involuntary movement
caused by prior expectations / or suggestions.

BEN. And in English?

LAUREN. We're moving the table, we just don't know / we are.

JENNY. No! I'm concentrating really hard on not moving it!

SAM. Right. And the harder you try not to do something, the
more likely you are / to do it.

BEN (*wound up, mocking him*). 'I think you'll find!' He's
making this up! / Fake news!

LAUREN. He's not.

> BEN *and* JENNY *look at her.*

> It's called White Bear Effect. Jenny, don't think of a white
> bear.

> *Beat.*

> Now all you can think of is white bears, right?

> JENNY *is swayed, torn.*

SAM (*triumphant*). Thanks, Loz. Let's call it a night. Hit the
lights.

> LAUREN *turns the anglepoise lamp on, shifting the
> atmosphere back to reality.*

JENNY (*to* LAUREN). But… you still believe?

> LAUREN *won't meet her eyes.*

> (*Desperate for solidarity.*) You saw your friend. Ida. The
> parakeets…

> SAM *shoots a looks at* LAUREN, *surprised* JENNY *knows
> about this.*

LAUREN. Oh, Jen… I believe my brain told me I saw her. But I
think it was wrong.

> JENNY *recoils.* SAM *moves towards her.*

SAM. It's over, Jen. Let's go / to bed.

She backs away, like a cornered animal.

JENNY. No! I felt it. Something travelled through my arms into / the table.

SAM. They're called nerves.

BEN. That's right, patronise / her again.

SAM. Stay out of this.

BEN. So you can bully your wife into agreeing with you?

LAUREN. Ben! Why don't you have a cigarette?

BEN. It's pissing down!

LAUREN. Now.

BEN. Or what? You going to hit me again?

She holds his gaze.

He relents, and walks towards the patio doors. As he opens the door, music plays – it sounds like a 1940s big-band number – woodwind and brass, eerie in its unexpectedness.

He turns and, like the others, looks towards the source of the music – Alexa. As a voice begins to sing, we recognise it as the song the 'old lady' taught BEN – 'In an Old Dutch Garden (By an Old Dutch Mill)' performed by Glenn Miller.

(Stunned.) It's my song!

SAM *walks towards Alexa, thrown.*

SAM. Stop the music.

The music does not stop.

JENNY. Alexa, stop the music.

ALEXA. Okay.

The music stops.

BEN. Believe, Jenny.

JENNY. I believe.

BEN *returns to the table and places* JENNY*'s hands on it.*

SAM. Get off my wife!

BEN. Or what, 'mate'?

He places his hands on JENNY*'s, his body against hers.*

Frank, are you still there?

The table moves.

SAM. Jenny!

BEN. Good old Frank. You and me, mate – the bottom fucking layer.

SAM. Jenny...

JENNY (*to Frank, almost trance-like*). Is it you walking in Phoebe's room?

The table doesn't move.

SAM (*to* BEN). I'm / warning you...

BEN. Is it another spirit?

The table moves – a sudden lurch.

SAM. You're doing / this!

BEN. Frank, is this spirit connected to somebody here?

The table lurches again, violently.

JENNY. I can't hold on.

BEN. Yes you can.

His body is trapping her at the table.

Someone in this room?

The table lurches again.

SAM. Jenny, please! / Let go!

BEN. Frank, can you move the table towards this person?

A long beat, then the table moves slowly towards SAM.

SAM. No...

(*Almost a guttural moan, to himself.*) You're doing it, / you're doing it...

LAUREN. Ben, stop this.

The table keeps moving until it reaches SAM. JENNY *and* BEN *now face him.* JENNY *is weeping.*

SAM. Jenny... Please... We'll forget everything and go back to how we were. Just stop.

She looks at him for an agonised moment, then turns to BEN.

JENNY. Ask it.

BEN. Frank, are Jenny, Sam or Phoebe in danger?

SAM. I said stop!

A beat and then BEN *suddenly freezes, a look of horror on his face –*

BEN (*scared, appalled*). Oh God! Fucking hell, no!

LAUREN. Ben?

BEN *pulls his hands away and the table flips over.*

Simultaneously, the anglepoise lamp falls with a smash, as some moving 'thing' collides with it, plunging the room into darkness.

JENNY. What was that? There's something here!

The 'thing' veers into the coffee table, knocking Mister Bear over. He falls onto a lit candle – the white spirt ignites and he is set on fire.

LAUREN. Oh Jesus!

She throws her wine on it. It flares up even more. Through the monitor, Phoebe screams.

Shit!

JENNY (*distraught*). Phoebe!

She runs upstairs.

LAUREN. Alexa, turn the fucking lights on!

ALEXA. Okay.

The main lights come on. Phoebe's screams continue.

BEN *stands frozen, not listening. We hear* JENNY*'s voice through the monitor.*

JENNY (*offstage*). Darling! Please! It's okay!

LAUREN *runs and grabs a saucepan of water from the kitchen and throws it over Mister Bear. Phoebe is hysterical.*

Baby, what is it?

SAM *looks at the chaos brought to his pristine home – the smouldering Mister Bear, the upturned dining table, the felled lamp and the open patio doors with rain lashing outside… Violated, he moves furiously towards* BEN, *ready to hit him.*

Phoebe! Phoebe!

BEN *looks up. His expression, visibly shaken, stops* SAM *in his tracks.*

BEN (*soft, distressed*). I understand now. I'm sorry. I'm so / so sorry.

JENNY (*offstage*). Darling, stop!! Sam!!

SAM, *confused and thrown, runs upstairs.*

Pandemonium can be heard, Phoebe screaming at her loudest as JENNY *cries. We hear* SAM *enter the bedroom.*

Sam!! I can't stop her / crying!

SAM (*offstage*). Calm down, Jen! For God's sake, / stop!

JENNY (*offstage*). Something's been in here.

LAUREN *watches as* BEN, *dazed, walks towards the patio doors.*

SAM (*offstage*). Jenny…

JENNY (*offstage*). Look!

SAM (*offstage*). Oh my God – (*To the 'thing'.*) Get out!

BEN *walks out into the garden. The security light springs on. Phoebe is still screaming.*

JENNY (*offstage*). Is it still in here?

> LAUREN, *confused, stares out at* BEN, *standing, head bowed, in the torrential rain*.

Is it here?

> LAUREN *picks up the baby monitor and turns it off*.

> *Snap to black*.

Scene Six

The clock races forwards to 02:12.

Lights up.

There are muddy prints across the white rug. The patio door is now closed. JENNY *is on the sofa, holding Phoebe, wrapped in a blanket*.

SAM. He must have run in when Ben left the door open.

JENNY. That smell…

SAM. He pissed in the hall. Bloody fox.

JENNY. It could have got into / her cot.

SAM. It didn't.

> *He puts his hands on her shoulders*.

> (*Trying to reassure*.) Everything can be –

JENNY. Explained?

> (*Shivers and moves his hand*.) Your hands…

SAM (*rubbing his hands to warm them*). You know what they say – cold hands, warm heart. Though I'm not sure there's any scientific basis to that.

> (*Surveys the rug*.) We're going to need one of those / steam cleaners.

JENNY. I don't want us to have another child, Sam.

A shocked beat.

Not in this house.

SAM, *stunned, searches desperately for something to say.*

I've called my parents. They're expecting us.

He sits next to her.

SAM. I love you.

JENNY (*sadly, tears welling*). No. You love what you made me. But I… I want to know if the old me is still there, under all the layers of you.

She places her head against his. They're both crying.

I want to be more than just a sponge.

SAM. We can talk about it. I promise… I promise I'll listen.

There's a knock on the patio door, breaking the moment. The security light springs on. LAUREN is illuminated by the door. BEN is further away, smoking, his back to the house.

JENNY opens the door and LAUREN enters.

LAUREN. Hi.

JENNY (*flatly*). Hi.

LAUREN looks at the clock.

LAUREN. So are we still doing this?

JENNY. Yes.

She gets up, holding Phoebe.

SAM. What are you doing?

JENNY. I'm putting her in her room.

LAUREN. Are you insane?

JENNY (*to* SAM). If I can prove to you this thing is here, if you can hear it too, then maybe there's hope. We can all leave this fucking house.

She exits upstairs with Phoebe. LAUREN *looks out towards* BEN.

LAUREN. Ben's being weird. He won't come in.

SAM. I hope he feels guilty. Bullshitting bastard.

LAUREN. One last drink?

She pours herself a glass of wine.

Oh, I forgot. You're still steely sober.

She sets the bottle down.

How's it been? Watching the rest of us get drunk and emotional? You get off on that?

She takes a big gulp. She's very drunk now.

SAM. Are you going to see him again?

LAUREN. I don't have much choice. He lives with me.

(*Off* SAM*'s surprise.*) After he did my bathroom, he never really left.

SAM. And you're okay with that?

LAUREN. Ghosts aren't the only thing that fills the gaps.

(*Then.*) Alexa, play Sam's dinner-party playlist.

ALEXA. Okay.

Alexa plays music – Portishead again, now a little eerie.

LAUREN (*re: Alexa*). She still not speaking to you?

SAM *shrugs morosely.* LAUREN *sits on the sofa.*

I read somewhere that humans are a species in transition. We're caught between rational machines and irrational beliefs.

(*Sips.*) Same thing, though, aren't they? Physics, ghosts, love, kitchen extensions. Writing books. It's all a distraction. To make us forget that life is pointless and death is final.

Beat.

Or is it?

She picks up the charred body of Mister Bear from the coffee table.

'We're going on a bear hunt.' You never did tell us how it happened.

SAM. I'm working on it.

LAUREN. You're running out of time, Sherlock…

She takes a sip of wine and sits back.

SAM. There is one explanation.

LAUREN. Yeah?

SAM. It was you.

LAUREN (*a tremor in her voice*). What?

SAM. You put the white spirit on him.

LAUREN. That is insane.

But she won't meet his eyes.

SAM. It's the opposite. If we rule out the impossible, it's the only sane way it could have happened. I think you took it in there, and then came out pretending you'd found it.

LAUREN. Why?

SAM. Some weird solidarity with Jen? Prove her ghost exists, even if it means cheating?

LAUREN (*beat; then*). I don't give a shit about her ghost. It was for you. I wanted to show you you could be wrong.

Long beat as they look at each other.

I've waited a long time, Sam. Even sat through your wedding thinking, the lightning, that's an omen, right? I kept believing, one day, you'd realise you made a mistake. That all those questions you like to ask… I was the answer.

SAM. I didn't know.

LAUREN. Sure you did. You know everything.

(*Glances at the clock.*) Funny, sitting watching the clock tick down. Been doing that for years, cos I couldn't bear the idea of being with someone nearly right. Having kids, knowing I didn't love them as much as I loved you.

Beat.

But time runs out. And now, all the nearly right people have found someone too. And you know how I feel, looking in on you all? The weddings, house-warmings, christenings, dream homes? I feel like Ida in her glass elevator, staring out, knowing it's over.

(*Then.*) I told you about her that night at the union because I loved you, and I thought you'd understand. And I only got drunk afterwards. Because you laughed at me. Been doing it ever since.

She downs her wine and stands up, but she loses her balance. SAM catches her as she falls. She's in his arms now.

We can hear JENNY coming down the stairs.

SAM. What if I said I was wrong?

LAUREN (*smiles sadly*). Too late, Sammy. I think you'll find.

She moves away from him as JENNY enters.

The clock says 02:19.

JENNY. Three minutes.

LAUREN. Alexa, stop the music.

ALEXA. Okay.

The music stops. JENNY turns the baby monitor on.

JENNY. I'm standing on the stairs.

(*Crossing to the door.*) I'm grabbing Phoebs as soon as you hear it.

SAM (*almost telling himself*). Nothing will happen. Things cannot appear and disappear.

JENNY *is about to exit, then, suddenly – the loud shrill of the doorbell.*

JENNY. Who the hell is that?

The security light comes on in the garden, illuminating BEN.

(*Warily.*) I'll go.

She walks into the hall and opens the front door, the chain is on.

(*Offstage.*) Hello?

PC MILLER (*offstage*). Jenny Marshall?

JENNY (*offstage*). Yes.

PC MILLER (*offstage*). I'm so sorry to call this late. My name's PC Miller and this is PC Stirling.

JENNY (*offstage*). Oh.

PC MILLER (*offstage*). Can we come in?

JENNY (*offstage*). Sure…

She undoes the chain and lets them in.

Sorry… You just…

She walks back into the room, followed by the two police officers, PC MILLER *and* PC STIRLING. *They're wet from the rain.*

I mean I thought you'd just call me.

PC MILLER (*surprised*). You've been expecting this?

JENNY. Yes. But I should never have phoned you. My problem, it's not something you can / help with.

PC STIRLING (*confused*). Mrs Marshall, would you like to take a seat, please? We've… erm… been contacted by a police team on Sark.

JENNY. Pardon?

PC STIRLING. The island where your husband was staying.

JENNY. Has he done something wrong?

PC MILLER. It seems he was involved in an accident.

JENNY. Oh my God! Has he… hurt someone?

(*A horrible realisation.*) Is / that what this…?

PC MILLER. It's worse than that. There's no easy way to say this. Sam is dead.

A shocked beat. JENNY *laughs.* LAUREN *joins in.*

(*Thrown.*) Mrs Marshall?

JENNY. Sam is here.

PC STIRLING. Pardon?

JENNY. He's…

She looks around and she and LAUREN *realise* SAM *is no longer in the room – no one's quite sure when he left.*

There's a sudden knock on the glass of the patio door. They jump.

Oh – he went outside.

She opens the door. The security light springs on as BEN *walks in, looking haunted. The garden is empty.*

BEN. I'm so sorry, Jenny.

JENNY (*confused*). What have / you done?

PC MILLER. I know this is very difficult, Mrs Marshall.

JENNY (*resisting vehemently*). No!

PC STIRLING. We believe he fell from a cliff, whilst walking at night.

JENNY (*shouts into the hall*). Sam!

PC STIRLING. It happened on a remote part of the island.

JENNY (*shouts again*). Sam!

PC MILLER. It's taken several days to discover him.

PC STIRLING. Four, we think.

JENNY (*gasps*). No!

LAUREN. Oh God!

JENNY (*voice rising, trying to stay calm*). That's not possible. He's been here / with us!

LAUREN. We had dinner…

PC MILLER (*confused*). He ate with you?

JENNY. Well, / he…

LAUREN (*remembering*). He didn't eat anything.

JENNY (*to* BEN). Where is he?

> *She runs into the garden.* LAUREN *lifts up* SAM*'s whiskey mug.*

LAUREN (*to herself, a sickening realisation*). Or drink…

> *Outside,* JENNY *shouts into the night.*

JENNY. Sam!

LAUREN. / No, no…

> LAUREN *runs into the hall and up the stairs, as desperate as* JENNY.

LAUREN. Sam!

JENNY (*urgently, panic creeping in*). Sam!

> *We hear the foxes reply.* JENNY, *startled, slips and fall into the mud of the garden.*

> (*Desperate, frantic now.*) Sam!!

LAUREN (*offstage, from upstairs*). Sam!

> JENNY *returns from the garden, soaked and covered in mud.*

JENNY (*distraught*). He's here…

PC MILLER. I know it's very hard to take in…

> LAUREN *runs back in, weeping.* BEN *reaches for her, but she pulls away, inconsolable.*

JENNY. No! You're wrong!

PC STIRLING. He had photo ID on him, and his phone.

PC MILLER. If it's any consolation, the last call he tried to make was to you, early Wednesday morning, timed at...

She consults her notebook.

JENNY (*cutting her off – a stunned, awful whisper*). 2:22.

The clock changes to 02:22.

Through the baby monitor, we hear the sound of footsteps in Phoebe's room.

JENNY *looks to the monitor.*

PC MILLER. Mrs / Marshall...

JENNY. Sssh!!

We focus in on the monitor as the footsteps walk round Phoebe's cot.

It's him.

Phoebe whimpers in her sleep.

Through the monitor, we hear the sound of a man crying. It is SAM; *uttering deep, heartbroken sobs.*

It was him.

The foxes let out one horrible final scream as the patio door inexplicably slams shut.

Blackout.

The End.

Author's Note

Shhh... Please don't tell!

Now you know the play's secret, keep it to yourself so others can enjoy the surprise too. The aim for any production should be that Sam passes through the entire evening leaving no physical imprint on the world around him, other than the sensation of cold he seems to engender when he's close to people. He does not eat, drink, or move any objects, but... this should only be obvious after the play has finished, leaving the audience to think back and recall the clues laid throughout. As I said in the introduction, a haunting is a detective story and that is definitely true of this one.

Acknowledgements

Thank you to Isobel David, Tristan Baker and Charlie Parsons at Runaway Entertainment for believing in the play, Matthew Dunster for his wisdom and talent, Jack Bradley for his mentorship and Shaparak Khorsandi and Ciaran O'Keefe for some key bits of real-life inspiration. Huge thanks to the brilliant original cast – Lily Allen, Julia Chan, Hadley Fraser and Jake Wood and Richard Pryal & Bianca Stephens, and to Jessica Ronane for bringing them together.

Thanks to Rosalind Grainger, Tom Ridsdale, David Langham, Peregrine Andrews, Michael Shaw, Rob Streeten and Tyronne Mann for answering questions during my research, and to Hannah Price, Carrie Cracknell, Sonia Friedman, Hugo Young, Francesca Devas, Rufus Wright, Sam Alexander, Mel Hudson, Anna Wheatley, Thomas Coombes, Sarah Ridgeway, Aoife Hinds, Tony McGeever, Jamie Mullan, Jenny Shaw-Sweet and Rose O'Sullivan for the various ways they helped or supported me during the play's development.

Finally, a big thank you to everyone who has told me about their ghostly experiences over the last few years – it takes bravery to say those words 'I have seen a ghost' and I feel privileged that you shared your stories. If you're reading this and want to tell me your own personal ghost story, or what you think of the play, you can email me – danny@dannyrobins.com, or find me on social media.

D.R.

www.nickhernbooks.co.uk

facebook.com/nickhernbooks

twitter.com/nickhernbooks